POWER UP!

Other Kaplan Power Books:

Kaplan Math Power

Kaplan Word Power

Kaplan Writing Power

Kaplan Learning Power

GRAMMAR POWER

THIRD EDITION

by Jane Schwartz

Simon & Schuster

NEW YORK · LONDON · SYDNEY · TORONTO

Kaplan Publishing
Published by Simon & Schuster
1230 Avenue of the Americas
New York, NY 10020

For bulk sales to schools, colleges, and universities, please contact Order Department, Simon & Schuster, 100 Front Street, Riverside, NJ 08075. Phone: (800) 223-2336. Fax: (800) 943-9831.

Contributing Editors: Seppy Basili and Trent Anderson
Project Editor: Ruth Baygell
Interior Page Production: Michael Wolff
Production Manager: Michael Shevlin
Production Editor: Maude Spekes
Cover Design: Cheung Tai
Editorial Coordinator: Déa Alessandro
Executive Editor: Del Franz

Manufactured in the United States of America
Published simultaneously in Canada

March 2003
10 9 8 7 6 5 4

ISBN 0-7432-4112-6

TABLE OF CONTENTS

ABOUT THE AUTHOR

Jane Schwartz taught writing for ten years at the college level, covering everything from scriptwriting to basic composition, essay, fiction, and business writing. She has also worked as a journalist and editor. She is the author of *Caught* and *Ruffian: Burning from the Start*.

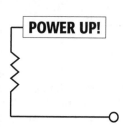

Getting Charged Up about Grammar

Most likely, you've picked up this book for one of two reasons: Either a teacher, adviser, or boss has decided that you need to brush up on your grammar skills, or you have decided the same thing for yourself. Maybe you're preparing for college and feel a bit shaky about your skills; maybe you're re-entering the work force and lack confidence in your written work. In any case—willingly or unwillingly—you've taken the first step and are reading this introduction. And you're already starting to feel that old, familiar dread.

WELCOME TO THE CLUB

You're not alone. You're part of a long tradition of people who were taught to view grammar as a vicious watchdog, poised in front of the House of English, ready to rip out your throat (or, at the very least, humiliate you in public) if you said or wrote anything that upset him.

The trouble is—if you're like most people—you can't always remember exactly what it is that gets Fido so mad:

Are you forbidden to ever split an infinitive?

Is a preposition a terrible thing to end a sentence with?

Or a fragment?

If you don't get these little grammar jokes (What? You didn't know there were grammar jokes?), you will after reading the pages to come.

In the meantime, try to forget your past encounters with the snarling beast. We've taken him to obedience school, and you can relax: This time the dog isn't going to bite. In fact, he's actually quite friendly. And he can be extremely useful because he knows everything about grammar. That knowledge is the source of his power. Kaplan has devoted this book to one simple task: transferring that power from the dog to you.

BE A GRAMMAR KNOW-IT-ALL

We'll explain in a minute how we intend to accomplish this amazing transfer of power (we can assure you that no animals were hurt or killed during the writing of this book), but first let's dispense with your two most burning questions on the subject of grammar: "Just what is it, anyway?" and "What the #@%#* do I need it for?"

What is grammar, anyway? Think of language as a game. You participate in this game every day in one or more (and frequently all) of the following ways: listening, speaking, reading, writing. *Grammar is simply the rules of the game.*

Every game has rules. In fact, almost every activity that you do is governed by some kind of rules. These rules range from formal laws to mere guidelines, and they apply to driving a car, baking a cake, playing baseball, designing buildings, greeting customers, launching a rocket, using the telephone, making a movie, or making a date. Even something as individual as raising children has "rules." (That's how Mr. Spock—the pre–*Star Trek* Mr. Spock—earned his reputation.)

Why do I need to know it? You need grammar for the same reason you need rules for the road: to help you arrive at your destination (clear communication) as smoothly and efficiently as possible, and to avert disasters, collisions, and injuries. Just as we have one set of rules for everyone who drives, we have one set of rules for "standard English," which just means English that conforms "to established educated usage in speech or writing." (*American Heritage Dictionary*)

KAPLAN

Good News/Bad News

You've got a lot going for you when it comes to language; you're not exactly a novice. You've been playing this game in some form (again, either listening, speaking, reading, or writing) every day of your life. Most of the time, in most of these activities, you don't even think about what you're doing. Most of the time, you manage to make yourself understood. So, the good news is—you obviously know most of the rules, whether or not you can explain them.

The bad news is . . . the rules you don't know are the ones that will inevitably get you into trouble. They'll cost you points on the SAT; they'll hinder your performance in college; they'll create a poor impression on the job; they'll cause misunderstandings in your personal life.

Read the following sentences:

1. Looking radiant in my new dress, my boyfriend insisted on taking me to the Rainbow Room.

    (Hey, we don't care if the guy's a cross-dresser, but if you write this sentence in a letter to your parents, they may get the wrong idea.)

2. The world would be a better place if we would just except everyone. (Maybe so, but then who'd be left?)

3. He loves you as much as I. (Does he love both of us, or do we both love you?)

Grammar Whys. Why do you have to follow the rules of "standard English"? Why isn't the English you use at home or with friends, the English of rappers and rock stars, comedians and cyberpunks, okay? Well, guess what? It *is* okay. It's okay in the same way that it's okay to wear a bathing suit at the beach but not at a fancy restaurant. Some kinds of clothing are appropriate for one occasion, but not for another. That doesn't make one outfit "good" and another "bad." It just means you have to make a choice.

Do you speak the same way to your parents as you do to your friends? The same way to your boss as you do to your neighbor? The same way to a date as you do to your brother or sister? Of course not. You automatically adapt your tone, style, and content to suit the situation.

That's all that standard English is: another outfit in your closet. But it is a very powerful outfit, as powerful as the magic slippers in *The Wizard of Oz*, because with standard English you can click your heels three times (actually, you don't have to click your heels at all—that was just in the movie) and go anywhere you want: the academic, business, and professional worlds are all open to you.

Using good grammar will not make you sound pompous, longwinded, or snobby (you can be pompous, longwinded, and snobby without knowing anything about grammar). On the contrary, grammar can help you sound clear, direct, and confident. It can help you say precisely what you mean to say. It allows you to be in control of your message, not the other way around. That's what we mean by "grammar power."

HOW TO USE THIS BOOK

How you use *Kaplan Grammar Power* depends on your goals.

First, here's how NOT to use this book:

- Do not read it in one sitting as though it were a novel.
- Do not try to memorize a list of all the rules.

The secret here is to learn some guidelines and then become familiar enough with the danger zones so that you'll recognize them. Once you know the potential pitfalls, you have one of the following options: (1) You can try to avoid them, (2) You can return to this book for help when you come to them, or (3) You can use this book to learn to conquer them (this will produce the best long-term results).

Make sure you read the first chapter on sentences. The sentence is the fundamental unit of communication, and every subsequent grammar topic will refer to what you have learned in this chapter. Make sure you understand the essential parts of a sentence and what their functions are. Review the most common errors in sentence structure and ways to correct them.

From then on, you have a choice: You can proceed in order through the book, studying each topic, or you can skip from chapter to chapter, subhead to subhead, to find help with specific practical problems as you encounter them in your own writing. Building grammar power is like building muscle power in the gym: some people will want to develop their biceps; others will concentrate on their abs; still others will want to improve the overall strength of all the major muscle groups.

Kaplan has done several things to make it easier for you to use this book in your own, individual fashion. In the back of the book you'll find a Glossary explaining grammatical terms. The Glossary cross-references these terms with their functional or everyday descriptions in case you can't remember what something is called (thus, "verbs" are also listed under "action words"; "gerunds" under "-ing words"; "infinitives" under "to + verb"). Once you find the correct term for something, you can use the cross-references to locate all the applicable discussions of this term in the book and go directly to them.

To help you focus, we have included a *Plug In* exercise at the beginning of each chapter. If you make mistakes or feel unsure during the *Plug In*, then take the time to study the chapter thoroughly and do all the exercises and activities. (Answers to all exercises can be found in Appendix A: Answer Key.)

If the *Plug In* is easy and you get all the answers right, you might decide to skim the chapter, subhead by subhead, quickly reviewing the material. In either case, do the exercises before going on. If you make any mistakes here, take the time to go back over the applicable sections of the chapter.

If you get all the answers right, your grammar battery has been successfully jolted and you're ready to proceed.

Appendix C includes a list of principal parts of irregular verbs that you can use for reference. Don't try to memorize them; just read through them once or twice to familiarize yourself with potential trouble spots.

In each chapter you'll find sidebars detailing exceptions to rules, tips for remembering important points, myths about language and grammar, bloopers, jokes, or fascinating facts. A *Power Surge* will provide you with strategies and tips. A *Power Line* will feed you famous (or infamous) lines from movies, books, or well-known persons to help illustrate to-die-for grammatical points. A *Spark* contains a tidbit of interesting information.

The point of increasing your grammar power is practical: to enable you to write and speak more effectively. So, no matter what we suggest, use this book in whatever way is most helpful to you.

WARNING!

Even if you read every chapter, do every exercise, and get all the right answers, your new-found knowledge of grammar is useless unless you can apply it in the real world. For the rest of your life, you'll be communicating—speaking and writing—in school, at work, and in your personal life. This communication is what connects you to other people, in every kind of relationship you can imagine.

That's the real reason for you to turn the page.

CHAPTER ONE

A Life Sentence

Read aloud the following group of words:

> He is a man who cares

Perhaps you read it this way:

> He is a man who cares.

But you might also have read it this way:

> He is a man. Who cares?

Both versions are grammatically correct, both make sense, and both use the same words in the same order. However, they convey two very different messages. To communicate your thoughts in a clear, unambiguous way, you need to structure your words into sentences. Individual words are important, but *meaning* comes from sentences.

PRACTICALLY SPEAKING

You've been using sentences to communicate for most of your life, so obviously you know a lot about them even if you can't name or identify a single part of speech. That's okay. You're not reading about grammar so you can discuss participial phrases on your next date (at least, we sincerely hope not!). You're taking time out of your busy schedule to study grammar for only one reason:

because it has practical value. *The practical value of grammar resides in making sentences.* That is its sole purpose. Communication—both verbal and written—is based on the sentence. That's why we're not going to spend the first 50 pages of this book teaching you the individual parts of speech. We're going to start right off with the real thing, what you use every day: the sentence.

The place to practice swimming is in the water, not on the shore. So jump in; the water's fine. (You will need to learn a few terms as we go along, but we promise to keep them to a minimum.)

Plug In

Sentences are made of subjects and verbs, some of which are part of a phrase or clause. In the following sentences, underline all subjects once and all verbs twice.

1. The phone is ringing.
2. Could you please answer it?
3. Don't tell anyone where I am!
4. Mom and Dad will not ground me; however, I will grind you up into little pieces in about two more minutes.
5. Having a little sister tries my patience.

SENTENCE POWER

What is a sentence? The sentence is our basic unit of communication. From it we build everything from news broadcasts to college application essays; from e-mail messages to research papers; from corporate memos to true-crime novels; from "Dear John" letters to instructions for taking medication. Plays and screenplays also grow from sentences (although, since they attempt to reproduce the spoken word, they do not always strive for grammatical correctness or completeness). Even poetry—no matter how the lines appear on the printed page—is carried, for the most part, on the backs of sentences.

What makes the sentence so powerful? A sentence is powerful because it is the expression of a complete and independent thought.

A sentence, standing all by itself, makes sense. Every sentence you write is like a minidrama or a very short story (the shortest story you can imagine): Someone (or something) *does* something (or *is* something). In other words: **Something happens.**

> The boy smiles.
>
> The girl swam.
>
> We are leaving.
>
> That movie was terrible.
>
> They endured.

In and of themselves, these may not be the kind of stories for which Nobel Prizes in Literature are awarded (although the last sentence comes from *The Sound and the Fury* by William Faulkner, who actually did win the Nobel Prize in Literature in 1949), but they each fulfill the basic requirements:

- Something happens.
- Someone (or something) does something (or is something).

SUBJECTS AND VERBS

You're already familiar with the basic elements of the sentence. You have an intuitive understanding of what goes where (most of the time). You can demonstrate this by writing an appropriate word in each space in the following sentences.

1. The _____ fell off the shelf.

2. _____ is my favorite food.

3. _____ are running in the halls.

4. An old _____ cannot always be repaired.

The words you wrote are *subjects*. Now write an appropriate word in each space in the following sentences:

5. Andrew and Jeff _____ with their father.

6. The teacher _____ the room.

7. The boys _____ less than the girls.

8. The key _____.

The words you wrote are *verbs*. To fulfill its storytelling requirement, a sentence must always have a *subject* and a *verb*, and it must be able to stand on its own.

What Is a Subject?

The *subject* is always some form of a *noun*. It is the actor in your drama.

- The actor doesn't have to be a person. It can also be a place, a thing, or an abstraction:

    The <u>desk</u> seems old.

    <u>Running</u> can be good for you.

    <u>Bombay</u> surprised me.

    The <u>future</u> remains a mystery.

    To <u>laugh</u> is to survive.

- The subject may consist of two or more separate actors. This is called a *compound subject*:

    <u>Kevin</u> and <u>I</u> fought constantly.

    <u>Eating</u> and <u>sleeping</u> were his favorite activities.

    <u>Men</u>, <u>women</u>, and <u>children</u> cried at this movie.

Exercise 1

Warmed up? Try this exercise. In each of the following sentences, underline the subject(s) once. (See the answers at the end of this book.)

1. We ran for the bus.

2. The roses smell wonderful.

3. January and February were the worst months of the year.

4. You frightened me.

5. To hear his voice gives me pleasure.

To Find the Subject. If you have trouble locating the subject, picture the drama in your mind. If you still aren't sure who the star of the sentence is, ask yourself what the action is. Once you see the action taking place, work backward and ask *who* or *what* is performing that action. That will be the subject.

What Is a Verb?

A *verb* is a word that shows action. It indicates what the subject *does* or *is* or *feels.*

- A single verb may be composed of more than one word: Jill <u>was running.</u>
- Negatives are not part of the verb: <u>I will</u> not <u>buy</u> that paper.
- When a subject performs two or more separate actions, you have a compound verb: Joyce <u>hacked</u> and <u>slashed</u> her way out of the forest.

To Check Your Verb Choice. If you're not sure about your choice for the verb, try putting *I, you, he, she, it, or they* before it and see if you get a sentence. If any one of those words fits, you've picked a verb. For example,

Being in pain isolates you.

Is *being* the verb? Use the test: "I being." "You being." "He being." "She being." "It being." "They being." None of these is a sentence; therefore, *being* cannot be the verb.

What other possible choice is there? *Isolates.* Try it out: "I isolates." No. "You isolates." No. "He isolates." BINGO! Therefore, *isolates* is a verb. (And, in case you're interested, that makes *being* the subject.)

Exercise 2

In each of the following sentences, underline the verb(s) twice.

1. He screamed at his younger sister.

2. Terry has been trying to buy a house.

3. Darryl sings in the chorus and plays on the football team.

4. We are not going to the party.

5. The painting lay in the closet gathering dust.

FOUR TYPES OF SENTENCES

Sentences can be classified according to purpose.

1. You can make a statement (*declarative sentence*).

I like my job.

2. You can ask a question (*interrogative sentence*).

Is Abigail your sister?

3. You can give a command (*imperative sentence*).

Sign the register.

What is the subject of this sentence? Hmmm . . . if you're baffled, try to picture the scene in your mind. The speaker is commanding someone to "sign the register." A command is an order given directly to someone. Therefore, the speaker is really saying, "You sign the register." The unwritten subject of a command is referred to as the implied or understood *you*.

4. You can express surprise or strong emotion (*exclamatory sentence*).

> What a day I had!

Although most sentences you write are declarative, it's good to know all four types so you can recognize them and use them to add variety to your work.

WORD ORDER

In statements, commands, and exclamations, the subject usually comes before the verb.

> The <u>crowd</u> <u>was</u> on its feet.
>
> <u>Stop</u> right there. (<u>You</u> <u>stop</u> right there.)
>
> How thrilled <u>I</u> <u>am</u> to see you!

In questions, the verb—or part of the verb—usually comes first.

> <u>Is</u> <u>Jason</u> at home? (<u>Jason</u> <u>is</u> . . .)
>
> <u>May</u> <u>I</u> see him? (<u>I</u> <u>may</u> see . . .)

When you speak, this is not necessarily the case. "I'm supposed to call him?" you might ask. But speech is different from writing: You can use your voice to create the questioning inflection, so you can take a declarative sentence and simply add the question mark with your voice. In formal writing, most questions start with a verb: "Am I supposed to call him?"

Here are some other variations on word order:

- You reverse normal subject-verb order when you begin a sentence with *there*, *here*, or *it*, as in the following examples.

> There <u>are</u> difficult <u>choices</u> in front of her. (choices are)
>
> Here comes the <u>judge</u>. (judge comes)
>
> There <u>are</u> many <u>opportunities</u> for you in this company. (opportunities are)
>
> It <u>was</u> terrible <u>weather</u> for rollerblading. (weather was)
>
> There <u>will be</u> another <u>train</u> in a few minutes. (train will be)
>
> There <u>is</u> no <u>reason</u> for you to make this mistake ever again. (reason is)

There and *here* are never the subject; when you place them at the beginning of a sentence, the verb will follow and then the subject. *It* can be the subject of a sentence, but only when it is taking the place of a specific noun.

You may choose to reverse normal subject-verb order to influence the rhythm of a sentence, to create suspense, or to add emphasis:

> Under the eaves <u>was</u> a <u>nest</u> of starlings.
>
> Faster and faster <u>ran</u> the <u>girl</u>.
>
> Thundering toward us <u>strode</u> the <u>giant</u>.

By putting the subject (actor) at or near the end of the sentence, you delay some revelation to the reader. If you have a reason for doing this, it can be an effective variation. If you don't have a reason for doing this, it can sound pretentious. ("To the professor's office go I.") The worst sin for a writer—apart from being unclear—is sounding pretentious!

Exercise 3

Pace yourself! In each of the following sentences, underline the subject(s) once and the verb(s) twice. Then, in the blank, identify the type of sentence: statement, question, command, exclamation. (Hint: A sentence can serve more than one purpose: "Don't hit her!" is both a command and an exclamation.)

1. Make my day. _____

2. Would you excuse me? _____

3. Please come here. _____

4. Stop right there! _____

5. There is no joy in Mudville. _____

CLAUSES AND PHRASES

If you learn to recognize clauses and phrases, you can avoid (or correct) the most common errors in sentence structure. You can also create more varied and interesting sentences.

What Are Clauses?

A *clause* is a group of words that contains both a subject and a verb. There are two types of clauses: Santa and Mrs. (Okay, okay.) Actually, as all Marx Brothers fans know, there's also the infamous "Sanity Clause." (Oh, okay!)

Seriously, the two types of clauses are independent and dependent clauses.

- An *independent clause* (also known as a main clause) is a group of words that contains both a subject and a verb and can stand on its own. Sound familiar? It should: This is how we defined a sentence. Therefore, you can conclude that a sentence is always composed of at least one independent clause.

  The ocean roared.

  Allison woke up.

An independent clause can stand by itself, join with another independent clause, or have a dependent clause attached to it.

- A *dependent clause* (also known as a subordinate clause or, during the Christmas season, as Santa's helper . . .) has a subject and a verb but cannot stand on its own. Why not? Because it has something extra, a word added at the beginning that destroys its independence. Any independent clause can be made dependent by placing one of the following words in front of it:

after	if, even if	when, whenever
although, though	in order that	where, wherever
as, as if	since	whether
because	that, so that	which, whichever
before	unless	while
even though	until	who, whom
how	what, whatever	whose

Try it for yourself. Take the following independent clause (sentence):

Rosie called her mother.

Add a word from the list:

Before Rosie called her mother.

Even though Rosie called her mother.

Since Rosie called her mother.

Because Rosie called her mother.

These are no longer independent clauses. Each has a subject and a verb, but they no longer make sense by themselves. The reader is left wondering, "Before Rosie called her mother, *what happened*?" or "Even though Rosie called her mother, *what happened*?" "Since Rosie called her mother, *what happened*?" "Because Rosie called her mother, *what happened*?"

Dependent clauses cannot stand on their own. The stage has been set, but no drama has unfolded!

What Are Phrases?

A *phrase* is a group of related words that does not have a subject and a verb. It might have one or the other, or it might have neither, but it doesn't have both. (If it had both, it would be a clause.) Here are some examples:

on the table	the funniest girl
tall, dark, and handsome	faster than a speeding bullet
which makes funny noises	to sing out loud
outrunning the competition	who was so kind

The most common type of phrase is the *prepositional phrase*. A preposition is a word used to show the relationship between two things, usually a relationship of place or time:

The dish is **on** *the table*.

She crawled **under** *the picket fence*.

He sits across **from** *me*.

The tree grew **between** *the two houses*.

She waited **for** *her trip* **to** *Mexico*.

A prepositional phrase consists of a preposition and a noun or pronoun, called the *object of the preposition*. The noun may have some modifying words around it. Take a moment to look over the following list of prepositions:

about	beside	of
above	between	off
across	by	on
among	during	onto
around	except	over

at	for	through
before	from	to
behind	in	toward
below	inside	under
beneath	into	with

There are three things you need to know about prepositional phrases.

1. **The subject of a sentence is NEVER in a prepositional phrase.** From now on, when you need to find the subjects and verbs in a sentence, the first thing you should do is draw a line through every prepositional phrase. This helps if you have a long sentence, as in this example:

    From the back of the freezing room in the old school, Cher, under three sweaters, sneezed into the tissue in her right hand.

Now cross out all the prepositional phrases:

~~From the back of the freezing room in the old school~~, Cher, ~~under three sweaters~~, sneezed ~~into the tissue in her right hand~~.

What you have left is the subject and the verb:

Cher sneezed.

This strategy also helps if you have a short sentence: The box of cookies was delicious. Which is the subject: *box* or *cookies*? The rule says the subject is NEVER in a prepositional phrase; therefore, you have to cross out *of cookies*:

The box ~~of cookies~~ was delicious. (*box* is the subject)

Crossing out prepositional phrases will help you find the essential parts of any sentence.

2. **A prepositional phrase, like any other phrase, cannot stand alone.**

3. **In general, try not to end a sentence with a preposition.** In olden days (that is, more than 20 years ago), standard usage dictated that you should *never* end a sentence with a preposition. Well, the guardians of the House of English have relaxed somewhat. (We told you Fido wasn't biting anymore.) Today, standard usage encourages you not to end a sentence with a preposition

> ⟨∿∿ **POWER LINE** ∿∿⟩
>
> This is the kind of English up with which I will not put.
>
> —Attributed to Winston Churchill

because it can sound awkward, especially in academic, business, or formal writing. For example:

A preposition is not something you usually want to end a sentence with.

But there are exceptions.

Fine: What's he good for?

Not: For what is he good? (sounds stilted)

Fine: What is that used for?

Not: For what is that used? (sounds too formal)

Fine: What do you keep your dirty laundry in? (sounds nosy, perhaps, but natural)

Not: In what do you keep your dirty laundry? (sounds nosy and snooty)

Remember, adjust your writing—as you would your clothing—so that it's appropriate for the occasion.

Don't be intimidated by long sentences. No matter how long or complicated a sentence is, it can always be reduced to its core: a subject and a verb. By weeding out the dependent clauses and prepositional phrases, you can find what is essential in any sentence. Conversely, you can develop your own sentences by starting with a core and adding information.

Earlier in the chapter, we gave you this sentence:

> The boy smiles.
> (Who or what is the actor? *Boy*. What does he do? He *smiles*.)

Let's expand the sentence:

> The boy who lives on the corner smiles.
> (Who or what is the actor? It's still the boy, but now we know which boy. What does he do? He *smiles*.)

Let's expand the sentence some more:

> The tall, extremely handsome boy who lives on the corner smiles.
> (Who or what is the actor? It's still the *boy*, no matter how handsome he is. What does he do? He *smiles*.)

Let's expand the sentence one more time:

> The tall, extremely handsome boy who lives on the corner smiles at me when I walk by.
> (Who or what is the actor? It's still the *boy*. What does he do? He still *smiles*, bless his little heart.)

Exercise 4

Keep breathing! In this exercise, you'll be finding subjects and verbs. In each sentence, underline the subject(s) once and the verb(s) twice.

In these sentences, the verb shows what the subject *does*:

1. Margot and Tony demanded a refund from the clerk who had lost their reservation.

2. I traveled through India.

3. When I go to my brother's house, his dog always jumps up and licks me on the face.

4. Sit down and make yourself at home.

5. Does Ruby yell at everyone?

In these sentences, the verb shows what the subject *is* or *feels*.

6. There were two reasons for Anna's resignation.

7. David is alone and seems sad today.

8. Ellen and Chris are my friends.

9. She does not appear sorry for what she did.

10. Where is everyone?

COMMON SENTENCE PROBLEMS

Now that you're familiar with the basic word groups (independent clauses, dependent clauses, and phrases) that make up sentences, let's see how problems arise. The most frequent problems in sentence structure are fragments and run-ons.

Fragments

A fragment is a piece of something. A *sentence fragment* is a piece of a sentence, either a phrase or a dependent clause. Avoid using fragments in any kind of academic, business, or professional writing—and in most other kinds of nonfiction writing as well. However, when you read novels, plays, screenplays, or poetry, you'll notice that fragments do appear, particularly when authors write dialogue or try to reproduce the natural rhythms of human thought.

Unintended fragments occur most often in the following situations:

- When you use dependent clauses:

  Rashid offered to buy the books. *Since he was going to the bookstore.*

  Before you sit down. Would you get me a cup of coffee?

- When you use -*ing* and *to* phrases:

  Jerry refused to give up the twenty-dollar bill. *Insisting it was his.*

  Jasmine left a note on the kitchen counter. *To remind her husband to feed the cat.*

- When you supply additional details (often beginning with words like *also, including, in addition, such as, for example, especially,* and *except*):

  Everybody criticized my screenplay. *Except the actor in the leading role.*

  Sam liked to try new foods. *For example, sushi and pickled plums.*

- When you supply additional actions:

  The doctor carefully examined my nose and throat. *Then looked inside my ears.*

  I had been playing tennis with my neighbor for several months. *And decided to invite him over for dinner.*

To Fix a Sentence Fragment. A fragment can be corrected by (1) attaching it to a sentence that comes before or after it, (2) adding a subject or verb to the fragment, and/or (3) changing the form of the verb to create a separate sentence.

Exercise 5

Go the distance! In the following fragments, either the subject or the verb or both are missing. First, state what is missing. Then, rewrite the fragment so that it becomes a complete sentence. Add capital letters and punctuation as needed.

1. trying to look out the window <u>subject and verb</u> (missing part)

   Rewrite: _____

   _____

2. a lot of cockroaches

    Rewrite: _____

    _____

3. and seems like a nice person

    Rewrite: _____

    _____

4. is nervous about the exam

    Rewrite: _____

    _____

5. one by one

    Rewrite: _____

    _____

6. in spite of all my efforts

    Rewrite: _____

    _____

7. after seeing the doctor

    Rewrite: _____

    _____

Rule Breaker

The following poem, "Harlem," was written by Langston Hughes.

> What happens to a dream deferred?
>
> Does it dry up
>
> like a raisin in the sun?
>
> Or fester like a sore—
>
> And then run?
>
> Does it stink like rotten meat?
>
> Or crust and sugar over—
>
> like a syrupy sweet?
>
> Maybe it just sags
>
> Like a heavy load.
>
> *Or does it explode?*

Now read the poem as it would appear in paragraph form:

> What happens to a dream deferred? Does it dry up like a raisin in the sun? Or fester like a sore—and then run? Does it stink like rotten meat? Or crust and sugar over—like a syrupy sweet? Maybe it just sags like a heavy load. *Or does it explode?*

This poem contains—gasp!—sentence fragments. Circle them. What is missing in each case: subject, verb, or both? Why do you think Hughes broke the rule for complete sentences? Is there a pattern to his rule breaking? Change the fragments to complete sentences according to the rules of standard English. Is the poem more or less effective? Why?

When you're in a rebellious mood and feel like breaking some rules, try writing a poem. It's a great way to experiment with sentence structure.

To Self-Check for Fragments. Check for fragments in anything you write by reading the piece aloud *from the last sentence to the first*. That way you can't fool yourself by automatically attaching a fragment to the sentence on either side of it, the way you might if you read the piece from beginning to end.

Run-Ons

A *run-on sentence* is one in which two independent clauses are run together without adequate signals (punctuation or a combination of a word and punctuation) to notify the reader that one thought has ended and another has begun. Writing a run-on sentence is like going through a red light. You know you're supposed to make a stop, but you don't.

Run-ons are divided into two categories:

- A *fused sentence* is one in which two independent clauses are run together with nothing—no word, no punctuation—separating them. (This is like speeding straight through the red light without even a pause.)

   The movie is good the book is better.

   The girls played baseball the boys went swimming.

- A *comma-splice sentence* is one in which two independent clauses are held together by placing a comma between them. A comma by itself is not strong enough to join two independent clauses. (This is like slowing down to see if anyone is watching and *then* going through the red light; it's a slight pause, but you're still breaking the law. Also, this is a rule that is broken often on the grammar road. Watch out for it. Don't be the one to get a ticket!)

   The movie is good, the book is better.

   The girls played baseball, the boys went swimming.

To Fix a Run-On Sentence. You can correct run-on sentences in one of three ways:

- Make the two independent clauses into two separate sentences.

  The movie is good. The book is better.

  The girls played baseball. The boys went swimming.

- Connect the two independent clauses with a comma and one of the following connecting words: *for, and, nor, but, or, yet, so.*

  The movie is good, but the book is better.

  The girls played baseball, and the boys went swimming.

  The girls played baseball, but the boys went swimming.

  The girls played baseball, so the boys went swimming.

(Notice that your choice of a joining word gives a slightly different emphasis to each of the corrected sentences.)

- Separate the two independent clauses with a semicolon. (Sometimes, one of the following connecting words may be used *after* the semicolon: *therefore, thus, however, nevertheless, also, furthermore.* If you use one of these connecting words in this way, it must be followed by a comma.)

  The movie is good; the book is better.

  The movie is good; however, the book is better.

  The girls played baseball; the boys went swimming.

  The girls played baseball; however, the boys went swimming.

Exercise 6

The following sentences have a variety of errors. First, state what the problem is (fragment, fused sentence, comma-splice sentence) in the space provided. Then do whatever is necessary to correct the sentence.

1. _____ After we woke up.

2. _____ That cute boy wearing the green sweater.

3. _____ I'm not going shopping, they never have what I want anyway.

4. _____ She brought her boyfriend flowers, candy wasn't good for him.

5. _____ He works hard on his papers he wants to get all A's.

6. _____ The dress doesn't fit, I'll buy it anyway.

7. _____ Sunshine is good for you too much sun is bad for you.

CHAPTER TWO

I'll Have Noun of It

Do you remember nouns? As you learned in the first chapter, a *noun* is a word that names a person, place, thing, or idea. In this chapter, you will learn more about what nouns are and the different ways they can be used in a sentence. You will learn to recognize different kinds of nouns and noun phrases, and you will learn more than you ever dreamed about plural nouns. First, let's look at the different types of nouns.

Plug In

Check out what you already know about nouns! In these sentences, do each of the following: 1) underline all nouns (including all words functioning as nouns) 2) add capital letters if needed and remove unnecessary capitals 3) correct any faulty plural nouns.

> ○⌁⋁⋁⋀∘ **POWER LINE** ∘⋀⋁⋁⌁○
>
> The beginning of wisdom is to call things by their right name.
>
> —Chinese proverb

1. To move to seattle would mean leaving a wonderful group of friend's.

2. Caitlin threw nora the bouquet.

3. Pablito, his only Grandchild, ran to greet him.

4. Her home is Brooklyn; she has lived in the Northern tip of that Borough for years.

5. Who was the idiot who let out the monkies?

COMMON AND PROPER NOUNS

A noun that names a class or type of person, place, thing or idea is called a *common noun*. Here are a few examples:

Her *friend* moved across *town* and joined a different *soccer* team.

A noun that names a unique or specific person, place, thing, or idea is called a *proper noun*. Proper nouns are always capitalized in English. The only other word we always capitalize is the pronoun *I*. (We'll get to pronouns in detail in chapter 4; they are the words that can take the place of nouns: *he, she, they, me, him, her, their, who*, etc.) Proper nouns are also called proper names.

Diane moved across *Houston* and joined the *Space City Kickers*.

Common Nouns	Proper Nouns
person	Aristotle
school	Howard University
war	the Civil War
state	Idaho
city	Baton Rouge
team	the New York Knicks
statue	the Statue of Liberty
country	Kenya
political institution	the House of Representatives
river	the Nile
award ceremony	the Academy Awards

Some words that are common nouns are capitalized when they become part of a proper noun (a name):

Example: I have three *aunts*.

But: My *Aunt Ellie* teaches yoga.

Example: My *high school* is closed this week.

But: *Clayton High School* has a new auditorium.

To Correctly Capitalize (Not!) Relationship Words. Don't capitalize words that name relationships (*mother, father, grandmother, uncle*). These are not proper nouns unless used as a name.

Example: I visited my *father*. (no capital)

This is like saying, "I visited my *friend*." My *father*, like my *friend*, states a relationship. (We have no idea what you actually call your father!)

In the following case, *Father* is the name you call your father. You could also write, "I visited *Daddy*." "I visited *Pop*." This is like saying, "I visited *Charles*." Other examples:

Example: I visited *Father* at work.

Example: When my *mother* arrives, we will drive to the coast.

But: When *Mom* arrives, we will drive to the coast.

Example: The boy wrote to thank his *uncle*.

But: "Dear *Uncle Leo*," the letter began.

To Capitalize or Not to Capitalize. You can lead the revolt against the Capital-ist Regime. Do not capitalize the following: seasons, professions, or directions. *Winter, spring, summer,* and *fall* begin with lowercase letters. Professions are not capitalized unless they are part of a title:

SPARK

In German, all nouns—both common and proper—are capitalized. If we did this in English, a typical sentence would look like this: When my Son sat in the Chair belonging to his baby Sister, She threw her stuffed Animal at his Head.

I studied with that *doctor*. My veterinarian is *Dr.* Bond. I can't stand that *professor*. Do you mean *Professor* Pinger? Directions are not capitalized: Go two blocks *north* and three blocks *east*. But the names of regions are capitalized: I live in the *Midwest*.

Exercise 1

Warmed up? Here's the first chance for you to exercise your noun power! Substitute a proper noun for the common nouns that appear in boldface. (Naturally, there's more than one correct answer.)

1. **My cousin** works at **an art museum.**   _____   _____

2. Have you read a **novel**?   _____

3. **The boy** went to see **the movie.**   _____   _____

4. Everyone in **the city** watches **the team** play ball.   _____   _____

5. **The song** came on the radio.   _____

6. **The professor** has stopped reading **the newspaper.**   _____   _____

Exercise 2

Here's another set of exercises! (Yes, already.) Now reverse gears and substitute a common noun for the specific proper noun given. (Again, there's more than one correct answer.)

1. *Star Wars* was released on videotape.   _____

2. The **Vietnam Memorial** draws thousands of visitors.   _____

3. Lora has been attending
   Brown University.

   _____

4. **Alonso** eats **Wheaties**™
   every morning.

   _____ _____

5. **Aunt Vicky** loves to teach
   third grade.

   _____

6. **Van Gogh** lives on through
   his paintings.

   _____

NOUNS WE KNOW AND LOVE

A *concrete noun* names something that has a physical reality. You can perceive it with your senses (sight, sound, smell, taste, touch): the *dog*, a *computer*, the *skyscraper*, the *blare* of the radio, the *odor* of onions, the *wind* (*wind* may seem abstract, but you can *feel* it and sometimes *hear* it).

An *abstract noun* names an idea, a state of being, or a quality: *justice, logic, hatred, passion, serenity, odds*. These are concepts that have no physical reality. You can perceive examples of them, or results caused by them, but you cannot see, smell, hear, touch, or taste a concept. For this reason, writers and artists often use metaphors to express abstract ideas. Example:

> Her serenity is a deep and calm lake.

We can't see serenity, but we can see the depth and calm of a lake. Artists also create physical images. We can't see "justice," but we understand how the image of a blindfolded woman holding a scale signals an unbiased weighing of both sides of an issue.

A *singular noun* names one person, place, thing, or idea (*boy, city, rock,*

∿∿ SPARK ∿∿

Sometimes concrete nouns also have an abstract meaning. Heart can be a concrete noun, a physical organ responsible for pumping blood throughout the body, but heart has also come to mean courage. Examples: Amy's heart was operated on. When tragedy befell her, she showed a lot of heart.

glory). A *plural noun* names two or more people, places, things, or ideas (*boys, cities, rocks, glories*). This is a very simple concept, but it has some tricky applications, as you'll discover later in this chapter.

Collective nouns name a group of people or things: *family, orchestra, jury, army, team, company, firm, class, corps, organization*. Because these nouns usually act as a unit, they are usually considered singular:

> The jury is entering the courtroom.

Verbs can also be nouns. Huh? Verbs are the wizards of the English language—they can change themselves into nouns. You probably recognize such nouns even if you don't remember the grammatical terms for them.

- The *-ing* form (gerund) of the verb can be a noun.

> *Running* in a marathon is difficult.
>
> He believed in *whistling* in the dark.

This is true only when the gerund appears by itself, without a helping verb in front of it. When a helping verb appears—Lulu *was running* the fashion show—the gerund remains a verb.

- The *to* + verb stem form (infinitive) of the verb can be a noun.

> To *run* in a marathon is difficult.
>
> He tried to *whistle* in the dark.

> ─⌁⌁○ **POWER LINE** ○⌁⌁─
>
> What we have here is a failure to communicate. (noun clause as subject)
> —from *Cool Hand Luke*

Noun clauses (Don't worry; we're not saying another word about You-Know-Who in the red suit . . .) are entire clauses that serve the function of a noun. (In the following examples, we've parenthetically indicated the uses for the noun clauses; these uses are explained in further detail in the next section.)

That is *what makes us human*. (complement)

She saw *that they were trying*. (direct object)

Give *whoever answers* the prize. (indirect object)

The money is for *whoever needs it.* (object of a preposition)

These ancient artists, *whoever they may be*, deserve respect. (appositive)

Whoever you are, welcome. (direct address)

NOUN USES

The *subject* of a sentence is always some form of a noun. It is the actor in your drama. In chapter 1, we also discussed nouns as the objects of prepositions, noting that a prepositional phrase always consists of both a preposition and a noun (*on* the *table*; *for* his *wife*).

There are other roles that nouns can play in a sentence. In fact, there are six main roles for nouns. Let's look at each function.

1. **Subject:** The actor in a sentence is the subject. It is always a noun, however simple or elaborate the sentence.

   <u>Stella</u> waved.

   The incredibly boring and longwinded <u>politician</u>, who had risen from the ranks in spite of many scandals and near indictments, continued his speech in spite of catcalls from the audience.

2. **Object of a Preposition:** The following are a few examples.

   John swings *at* the *ball*.

   Alice dropped *onto* her *knees*.

   Kip is writing *for posterity*.

   Jim cried *without embarrassment*.

3. **Object—Direct or Indirect:** In chapter 1, we said the sentence needed two elements: a noun and a verb. Something happens. Frequently, however, there are other parts of the sentence as well: Something happens *to* someone or something. That someone or something is a *direct object*.

> Ina uses *her computer* at work.
>
> The leopard devours *its prey*.
>
> The new boy stole *her heart*.
>
> Linda is writing *a novel*.
>
> The critic reviewed *the movie*.
>
> Alice dropped *the cake*.

Take this last sentence. But let's change it to show that Alice isn't clumsy; let's say she's generous.

> Alice gave John the cake.

At first glance you might be tempted to call *John* the object, because it follows the action word (the verb *gave*) but stop and picture the actual scene: Is Alice giving away John or the cake? She's giving away the cake; therefore, *cake* is the object of *giving*. But John is receiving something, too; he is receiving the cake. Thus, *John* becomes the *indirect object*, which means the person or thing receiving a direct object.

Even if you rephrase the sentence as a command—"Give John the cake."—or a question—"Have you given John the cake?"—*cake* is still the direct object and *John* the indirect object.

To Determine Direct and Indirect Objects. The direct object receives the action of the verb; the indirect object receives the direct object. Take the following sentence:

> Skip sent me a letter.

Letter is the direct object. *Me* is who receives the letter, so *me* is the indirect object.

Here's a simple test to see if a word is an indirect object. Put the preposition *to* or *for* in front of it and see if the sentence makes sense. If it does, you've got an indirect object. Take the earlier example:

Alice gave John the cake.

Alice gave John to *the cake.*

Alice gave the cake *to John.*

4. **Complement:** A sentence consists of someone or something doing or being something. *Doing* is covered in the above examples; the noun can be an action by itself or an action done to something else.

Sometimes, however, a verb doesn't show a physical action; it shows a feeling or a state of being. We call those words *linking verbs.* (More—lots more!—on verbs in the next chapter.) Linking verbs link the subject to a word on the other side of the verb. The word on the far side of the verb is called a *complement.* If that word is a noun, it's called a *noun complement,* and it renames or identifies the subject. (You don't have to remember these grammatical terms; just be familiar with the use of such nouns.)

Susan is *my sister.*

Brooklyn is *his home.*

5. **Appositive:** An *appositive* is a noun that appears, usually right after another noun, renaming or identifying the first noun. It's different from a noun complement because no linking verb intervenes to join the two nouns. The appositive can be taken away and the sentence still makes sense.

My sister, *the molecular biologist,* has arrived in San Antonio.

Sister is the subject; the writer has added *the molecular biologist* either to distinguish this sister from other sisters or to add identifying information the writer wants the reader to know.

Appositives can appear anywhere a noun can appear:

- *Subject*—The protagonist, *Stephen Dedalus*, goes on a journey.
- *Object of a Preposition*—He bought the ball for Jimmy, *his cousin.*
- *Direct Object*—They gave the basketball, *a birthday gift*, to Jerry.
- *Indirect Object*—She tossed Fido, *the grammar dog*, a bone.
- *Complement*—That is the writer *Grace Paley.*

6. **Direct Address**: Nouns are also used to name someone or something that we are speaking to directly.

> *Benjamin,* have you done your homework?
>
> Settle down, *class*!

Exercise 3

Whew! That was a long training session! Now, give those bulging grammar muscles a workout. How are the following nouns used in each sentence? Label each one: subject, object of preposition, indirect object of verb, direct object of verb, complement, appositive, or direct address.

1. <u>Sally</u> sallied forth.   _____

2. <u>Peanuts</u> are in the <u>bowl</u>.   _____ _____

3. Give <u>me</u> your <u>tired</u>, your <u>poor</u>.   _____ _____ _____

4. <u>She</u> threw <u>him</u> a <u>curve</u>.   _____ _____ _____

5. <u>Lillian</u> is a <u>comic</u>.   _____ _____

6. <u>She</u>, the <u>comic</u>, makes <u>us</u>
   all laugh.   _____ _____ _____

7. Go to <u>bed</u>, <u>child</u>!   _____ _____

PLURAL NOUNS

A *singular noun* names one person, place, thing, or idea. A *plural noun* names two or more people, places, things, or ideas.

To Form Most Plural Nouns. You form most plurals by adding *s* or *es* to the singular: *boys, monkeys, peas, dresses, foxes.* When a word ends in a -*y* that is not preceded by a vowel, you change the *y* to *i* and then add *es: ponies, phonies, babies.*

The dictionary will give you the spelling of irregular nouns (those that do not follow these rules), but you can familiarize yourself with many of the exceptions and categories below.

To Form Plural Nouns for Nouns Ending in *o*. You can usually make the plural form of nouns ending in *o* by adding *es: potatoes, tomatoes, tornadoes, mosquitoes, heroes, vetoes, cargoes.* But there are exceptions (the list is heavy on the musical instruments and terms): *radios, portfolios, tattoos, studios, rodeos, memos, photos, cellos, piccolos, pianos, tempos, virtuosos.* And here's one exception you'll recognize: the singular *graffito,* which we almost never use, becomes the widely known plural *graffiti.*

To Form Plural Nouns for Nouns from Other Languages. Oftentimes nouns borrowed directly from other languages maintain their original spellings: *medium/media; phenomenon/phenomena; stimulus/stimuli.* Sometimes they anglicize themselves by simply adding *s* to the singular: *memorandum/ memorandums; stadium/stadiums; plateau/plateaus; beau/beaus.*

To Form Plurals of Proper Nouns. Plurals of proper nouns generally follow the same rules as plurals for common nouns: You add *s* or, if a name ends in *s, sh, ch, x,* or *z* , you add *es:*

> The *Murrays* always made me feel at home.
>
> We don't keep up with the *Joneses.*
>
> Three *Januarys* ago, they traveled to Australia.
>
> Last year there were three *Charleses,* two *Janices,* and two *Lewises* in our class.
>
> The *Lopezes* and the *Husches* are old friends.

To Form Plurals of Hyphenated Nouns. If two or more words are joined by hyphens, add the plural ending to the main noun: *sons-in-law, daughters-in-law, mothers-in-law, fathers-in-law* (and other "in-laws"); *attorneys-at-law.*

To Form Plurals of Compound Nouns. If two words are joined to form a singular noun—*backyard, foreman, bucketful* (sometimes a letter is left off)—you form the plural by adding *s* or *es*, or, in the case of *foreman*, changing *man* to *men*. In other words, don't open up a closed word to make a plural. For example, do not write "two teaspoonsful of medicine."

If following the general rules for noun plurals results in awkward constructions, try rewriting the sentence. For instance, "The museum purchased three Matisses and two Velasquezes and two Grises." Ugh! A clever writer might recast the sentence to avoid such awkwardness. "The museum purchased three paintings by Matisse, two by Velasquez, and two by Gris."

Exceptions to the Plural Noun Rules: Some words are the same in both singular and plural form. An unusual percentage of them name animals: *deer, elk, sheep, fish, moose, swine, vermin.* Another example is the word *series*:

> The television *series* <u>is</u> interesting.
>
> Three new *series* <u>are</u> being premiered this week.

Some words change in weird and irregular ways: *child/children; man/men; woman/women; mouse/mice; ox/oxen; die/dice.*

Some words look plural but are singular in meaning (including some academic subjects, tools, diseases, and games): *economics, physics; scissors, tweezers, pliers; measles, mumps, herpes, AIDS; billiards, checkers, dominoes; molasses, whereabouts.*

Exercise 4

Here's a challenge for you. Find all the irregular plurals in the following titles, change them into singular nouns, and then make any additional changes you think necessary so that the new titles make sense.

All My Children _____

Days of Our Lives	_____
Little Women	_____
Of Mice and Men	_____
The Snow Geese	_____
"Autumn Leaves"	_____

Miscellaneous Plural Noun Situations

It's the English language, and there are always situations that aren't easy to categorize. Here are some plural noun oddities that are helpful to know.

To Form Plurals of Letters and Numbers. When you have letters and numbers (whether spelled out or in figures) used as nouns, you form the plural by adding s alone: *the three Rs, in twos and threes, IOUs, the early 1950s.*

To Form Plurals of Confusing Abbreviations and Letters. When you have abbreviations with periods, lowercase letters used as nouns, and capital letters that would be confusing if s alone were added, you form the plural by adding 's: *M.A.'s* and *Ph.D.'s, p's and q's, A's, I's, SOS's.*

Exercise 5

Still breathing? Hang in there—here's another set of noun sprints to increase your grammar power! The nouns in bold are all singular. Cross them out and change them to the plural form in the blanks provided.

The **Kennedy** (1)_____ and the **Martens** (2)_____ will be joining us for dinner. The latter own six racehorses and have won two Kentucky **Derby** (3)_____. The **daughter-in-law** (4)_____ always plan a skit for the holidays. "May all your **Christmas** (5)_____ be white."

THE LIVING LANGUAGE

Common usage influences what Fido the grammar dog will allow inside his gates. Over time, certain words that were once accepted fall out of favor, and other words take their place. This is also true of noun plurals. For example, the plurals of *fungus* and *cactus* used to be *fungi* and *cacti*, but now many dictionaries list those as second choices, after *funguses* and *cactuses*.

> ⌇⌇**POWER SURGE**⌇⌇
>
> When in doubt, check it out. If the dictionary lists two possible plurals for a noun, choose the first one.

Exercise 6

Underline all the nouns and then correct any errors in capitalization.

1. John saw his Aunt talking to his brother.

2. He liked aunt ida better than his other aunt.

3. When I'm bored with School, I think of transferring to the university of Michigan.

4. She is my best Friend.

5. I met her when I lived in missouri.

6. There are 50 States in the United States of America.

7. She wants to be a Doctor when she grows up—a medical Doctor, not a ph.d.

8. When I was in paris, I saw the eiffel tower.

9. Have you been to paris in the Spring?

10. April is often rainy there, but may is beautiful.

CHAPTER THREE

The Verb Circus: Under the Big Tense

The scene: a darkened theater, Anytown, U.S.A. The music begins, the curtain rises, a light goes up, and a single actor appears on stage. The audience is breathless with anticipation. Do you know what they are waiting for?

They are waiting for . . . the verbs.

Nothing *happens* without verbs. Verbs are the action words, the words that get things going. All the nouns in the world—even the most wonderful, precise, dazzling nouns—remain frozen, helpless, and immobile until you connect them to a verb. Verbs give life; they animate your sentences and conversations by expressing what someone or something *does* or *is* or *feels*.

Plug In

Let's see how much you already know about verbs with this opening quiz. Circle the correct form of the verb in parentheses.

Henry, along with his brother Kevin, (plan, plans) to surprise their mother for her birthday. She is usually so tired after work she has to (lay, lie) down and rest for half an hour before making dinner. What the boys have in mind (was, is) a home-cooked meal of their own.

"Where (are, is) the set of wine glasses?" (ask, asks) Henry.

"Most of the glasses (are, is) in the box, but one is (broke, broken)."

After (making, to make) hamburgers and baked potatoes, they call their mother. She is astonished. "I wish Daddy (was, were) in town to see what a beautiful job you've done!" Neither the boys nor their mother (try, tries) to hide their delight when they bring out the dessert. The dessert (are, is) ice cream sundaes.

ENTER THE VERB

Because verbs are so versatile and changeable, we use a standard form called the *infinitive* to identify them. The infinitive consists of the word *to* plus the verb stem: *to be, to run, to laugh, to see, to pick up, to write.*

Actually, as soon as the actor (subject) *appears*, you have your first verb. *Appear* is one of those quiet verbs: it doesn't *strut* or *fret* its hour upon the stage (Shakespeare's *Macbeth*, if you're trying to remember which play that phrase is from), but it's useful, as *are* many verbs. For in addition to showing overt physical actions (*action verbs*) verbs also *show* what someone or something *is* or *feels* (*linking verbs*).

If you're not sure which word is the verb, change the *time* of the sentence. The verb is the only word that changes its form to show the new time.

Original sentence:	I drive to work in my beat-up old car.
Yesterday:	I drove to work in my beat-up old car.
Tomorrow:	I will drive to work in my beat-up old car.
At this moment:	I am driving to work in my beat-up old car.

Drive must be the verb in the original sentence.

Action Verbs

There are two kinds of action verbs:

- A *transitive verb* transmits an action from the actor to the receiver, or direct object. In other words, in this kind of a sentence, someone (or something) does something to someone or something.

  <u>Noah</u> <u>hit</u> his sister.

  <u>She</u> <u>was kicking</u> the ball.

  <u>He</u> <u>recited</u> the poem.

  <u>I</u> <u>call</u> your name.

- An *intransitive verb* expresses an action that is not transmitted to an object. An intransitive verb does not need a direct object. It expresses an action without a receiver.

  Daisy <u>laughed</u>.

  Robert <u>screamed</u> for help.

  They <u>wept</u>.

(Remember, in the second example above, *for help* is a prepositional phrase, not a direct object; prepositional phrases can be removed from a sentence without changing the essential meaning.)

Many verbs can be both transitive and intransitive, depending on the situation.

Johnny Nolan <u>sang</u> beautifully. (intransitive)

Johnny Nolan <u>sang</u> his favorite song. (transitive: What did he sing? His favorite song.)

We <u>are running</u> late. (intransitive)

We <u>ran</u> the marathon. (transitive: What did we run? The marathon.)

Exercise 1

Warmed up on those action words? Here's a quick sprint, this chapter's first exercise! Draw a line across to the description that matches each verb.

1. The willow tree weeps.   Linking

2. The willow tree seems sad.   Transitive

3. The willow tree comforts me.   Intransitive

Linking Verbs

A *linking verb* links the subject of the sentence with a complement. A *complement* is a word on the other side of the verb that gives you more information about the subject itself. A complement can be:

   • Another noun, which *identifies* or *renames* the subject.

       David <u>is</u> *her cousin*.

       Ben <u>was</u> the captain of the water polo team.

   • A modifier, which *describes* the subject.

       Eddie <u>looks</u> *sad*.

       Claudia <u>is</u> brilliant in math.

       That cantaloupe <u>tastes</u> *delicious*.

Some linking verbs can also be used in the same sentence with action verbs:

       I tasted the melon, which <u>was</u> *delicious*.

And here are some other examples of linking verbs:

       That package <u>is</u> for you.

       Los Angeles <u>seems</u> unreal.

He <u>feels</u> confused.

Joey <u>was</u> not late.

Phrasal Verbs

Sometimes prepositions pair up with verbs (Get it? Pair *up*!). We call this type of verb a *phrasal verb* because the verb stem itself consists of two or more words, making it a phrase. The infinitive is to *pair up*.

We'll talk more about this in the chapter on idioms, but we mention it now so that you'll recognize verbs with more than one stem word. Here are some examples:

> The kids <u>turned out</u> the lights, <u>switched off</u> the radio, <u>clicked on</u> the TV, and <u>picked out</u> a video.
>
> "Well," said Mom, "at least they're not <u>running up</u> the phone bill."
>
> Dad laughed. "You're <u>putting</u> me <u>on</u>, right?"
>
> "I wouldn't <u>rule out</u> that possibility," smiled Mom.

SUBJECT-VERB AGREEMENT

Memorize the following rule exactly as it appears!

To Ensure Present Tense Subject-Verb Agreement. A singular subject takes a singular verb; plural subjects take plural verbs.

The preceding sentence not only states the rule; it illustrates it as well. Can you see how?

- Underline the subject of each independent clause once:

> A singular <u>subject</u> takes a singular verb; plural <u>subjects</u> take plural verbs.

- Now underline the verb in each independent clause twice:

A singular <u>subject</u> <u>takes</u> a singular verb; plural <u>subjects</u> <u>take</u> plural verbs.

The word *subject* is singular (one subject). The verb that goes with it is *takes*, which ends in an *s*. The word *subjects* is plural (more than one subject). The verb that goes with it is *take*, which has no *s* on the end.

This is one of the little ironies of English: The plural form of most nouns ends in *s*, but it is the singular form of the verb that ends in *s*. This rule generally applies to the *present tense* form of verbs. In all other tenses, which we'll get to shortly, there is no change in the singular and plural forms of the verb.

Here's another way to remember the agreement rule: In the present tense, when a subject is third person singular (a noun or the pronouns *he*, *she*, or *it*), the verb always takes an *s*. (If the term *third person* baffles you, take a peek at the next chapter.) Here are some examples of this "S Rule":

He <u>ropes</u> the calf.   They <u>rope</u> the calf.
(singular subject; verb needs an *s*)   (plural subject; no *s* on verb)

The girl <u>is</u> late   The girls <u>are</u> late.
(singular subject; verb needs an *s*)   (plural subject; no *s* on verb)

There are, of course, exceptions to every rule in English. Here are some of the notable subject-verb agreement exceptions:
- The past tense of *to be*: he *was*, they *were*
- The past tense of *to have*: she *has*, they *have* (Amazingly enough, the "S Rule" still applies.)

Tricky Stuff

Subject-verb agreement can be particularly challenging to speakers of English as a second language or to speakers who grew up speaking or hearing a *dialect* (a regional or ethnic variation) of English. So much of what seems "right" or "normal" about language depends on what we have heard all our lives. After all, we did not come into this world speaking or reading or writing—but most of us have been *listening* to the spoken word since birth (and maybe before!).

Even for speakers who normally have no problems with standard English verbs, there are certain situations that are a little trickier than usual. In the next few pages we will introduce your grammar muscles to the six stretches (rules for the road) necessary to get those tricky subjects and verbs agree!

To Ensure Subject-Verb Agreement with Multiple Noun Subjects. Here's what to do when you have more than one noun in the subject part of the sentence:

- If the word *and* joins the nouns, use the plural form of the verb.

    Mary *and* Bill <u>are</u> leaving at noon.

    She *and* I <u>operate</u> at different hospitals.

One Exception: When two different nouns refer to the same subject, use the singular form of the verb.

    My <u>friend and mentor</u> <u>operates</u> at this hospital.

You are speaking of only one person who is both *friend* and *mentor*; therefore, you need a singular verb. Here's another example:

    <u>Spaghetti and meatballs</u> <u>is</u> my favorite meal.

It's the combination, acting as a unit, that is your favorite meal. Other examples of subjects that look compound but function as a unit (singular) are "peanut butter and jelly," "peaches and cream," and "bacon and eggs."

Another Exception: When the word *every* or *each* is placed before two singular subjects joined by *and*, the meaning of the sentence is changed and requires a singular verb.

Example:	The sweater and skirt <u>have</u> their own hangers.
But:	*Each* sweater and *each* skirt <u>has</u> its own hanger.

When the word *each* is placed *after* a compound subject, however, it does not affect the plural verb form. (British English often considers this construction to be singular, but then, we're not in Great Britain, are we?)

The sweater and skirt each <u>*have*</u> their own hanger.

- If the following words or phrases join the two nouns—*as well as, along with, together with, in addition to, accompanied by*—use the singular form of the verb.

Mary, *together with Bill*, <u>is</u> leaving at noon.

(*Mary* alone is the grammatical subject. The phrase *together with Bill* adds information but is not essential to the main idea and could be removed: Mary is leaving at noon.)

If the word *or* joins the nouns, use the singular form of the verb.

Mary or Bill <u>is</u> leaving at noon. (Only one person is leaving.)

If the constructions *either . . . or* and *neither . . . nor* join the nouns in the subject, the verb agrees with whichever noun is closer to the verb.

Either the students *or* the teacher <u>is</u> leaving at noon.

Neither the teacher *nor* the students <u>are</u> leaving at noon.

To Ensure Subject-Verb Agreement with Certain Pronouns as Subjects. Here's what to do when vague or general pronouns are used as subjects:

- If the subject is *either, neither, each, someone, anyone, somebody, anybody, nobody, everybody*, or *everyone*, use the singular form of the verb.

Everyone <u>is listening</u> to the teacher.

Nobody <u>is listening</u> to the teacher.

Someone <u>has</u> a friend.

Everybody <u>has</u> a friend.

- If the subject is *few*, *many*, *both*, or *several*, use the plural form of the verb.

    Few are paying attention.

    Many are paying attention.

- If the subject is *some, any, most, all*, or *none*, you have a choice. (We'll refer to these as "choice" words.) These words will usually be followed by *of*. Look at the word after *of* and decide if it is one unit or a collection of individual items.

    Some of the cake is missing. (a cake is a unit and therefore singular)

    Some of the cookies are missing. (cookies are individual items and therefore plural)

Occasionally, the *of* phrase is left out; then you must look at the context, usually the previous sentence or independent clause, to find out what the pronoun—*some, any, most, all, none*—is referring to:

    The visitors were here for a week, but now *all* [of them] have gone.

    The roast was delicious; *none* [of it] is left for tomorrow.

Many language experts refer to nouns as either *count nouns* (individual items that can be counted, like *visitors* in the first example above) or *noncount nouns* (a single unit or mass, like *roast* in the second example). If you remember to form a mental picture, you won't have to learn any terms: If you visualize lots of individual items or pieces, you'll see "things" and know they are plural; if you see one unit, you'll visualize "a thing" and know it's singular.

To Ensure Subject-Verb Agreement when Subject Nouns Precede an *of* Phrase. When you have a noun followed by an *of* phrase: The verb agrees with the word before the *of* unless the word immediately before the *of* is a "choice" word (see above). If that's the case, you have to decide if it is singular or plural.

    The package of cookies is missing.

    Most of the meal has already been eaten.

Here's a flashback to chapter 1. The subject of the sentence is never found in a prepositional phrase. *Of* is a preposition, so the *cookies* couldn't be the subject of this sentence. *Package* is the subject, and it is singular. For the second sentence, *most* is a choice word, so you have to decide if it's one unit or a collection.

To Ensure Subject-Verb Agreement within Certain Word Groups. When you have word groups beginning with the pronouns *who, whom, whose, which,* and *that*, the verb agrees with the word immediately before the pronoun.

> The leader of the men *who <u>are</u>* tired is unwilling to rest.

Who is the pronoun; immediately before it is the word *men*. *Men* is plural, so the verb for this clause must be plural: *are*.

To Ensure Subject-Verb Agreement when Sentences Begin with Certain Words. What do you do when a sentence begins with *there, here,* or *where*? The verb agrees with the noun or pronoun that follows the verb, because that noun or pronoun is the subject of the sentence. (*There, here,* or *where* are never the subjects.)

> Here <u>is</u> the boy.
>
> Where <u>are</u> the <u>children</u>?
>
> There <u>are</u> no simple <u>solutions</u>.
>
> There <u>is</u> no simple solution.

To Ensure Subject-Verb Agreement When a Verb Links Two Nouns. When a verb links two nouns, the verb agrees with the subject of the sentence, not with the complement.

> The <u>problem</u> <u>is</u> the mice.

Problem is the subject, so it is singular. *Mice* is the complement; the fact that it is plural does not affect the verb.

> The <u>mice</u> <u>are</u> the problem.

Mice is now the subject; it's plural, so we need a plural verb, *are*. The complement is now *problem*, which doesn't affect the verb.

Here are a few more helps for miscellaneous tricky cases:

- When the subject is a title (of a book, movie, song, etc.), it is considered singular and takes a singular verb.

   Star Wars <u>occupies</u> a unique place in film history.

   The Sound and the Fury <u>is</u> an unforgettable novel.

- When the subject is a quantity (of money, time, space), it is singular:

   <u>Twenty-three dollars</u> <u>is</u> the price.

   <u>Eighteen inches</u> <u>is</u> the width of the cloth.

   <u>Three-quarters</u> of the class <u>has been</u> absent with the flu.

   But: <u>Three-quarters</u> of the students <u>are</u> sick. (*Three-quarters* functions like the "choice" words—see page 45. *Class* is a unit; *students* are individuals.)

- When the subject looks plural but is singular in meaning, it is singular:

   <u>Physics</u> <u>is</u> my favorite subject.

   <u>AIDS</u> <u>remains</u> a devastating disease.

   <u>Measles</u> <u>takes</u> a toll on children.

   <u>Checkers</u> <u>is</u> still a popular game.

- When the subject is a collective noun (acting together), it is singular:

   The <u>jury</u> <u>decides</u> an important case.

   My <u>team</u> <u>wins</u> on the road and at home.

Exercise 2

In each of the following sentences, circle the correct verb.

1. The teachers in the most rundown school building (is, are) dedicated to the students.

2. Where (was, were) the doctors when the casualties started coming in?

3. Most of the meal (has, have) already been eaten.

4. Some of the candies (is, are) gone.

5. Everyone usually (pushes, push) to the front of the line.

6. Anna, with some help from her friends, (is, are) organizing a chorus for the seventh grade.

7. Neither Bob nor his brothers (lie, lies).

8. A bushel of apples (was, were) waiting on his front porch.

9. The boy with the six adorable puppies in his arms (run, runs) the pet store.

THE BIG TENSE

Time is divided into past, present, and future, and so are verb tenses. These categories are further divided so we can express all kinds of fine distinctions in time. There are *twelve* tenses altogether, but don't panic! You already use them all (some more than others, of course). We include one example below so you can remind yourself how many different shapes verbs can assume. Look over the different tenses, but don't drive yourself crazy trying to memorize terms.

When you see the term *perfect* in the name of a verb tense (see our handy table of examples), it will help if you think of it as meaning "completed." When you see the term *progressive*, think of it as meaning "continuing."

TENSE	EXAMPLES
Present	I *play*. He *plays*. Do they *play* music?
Past	I *played* tennis this morning. He *played* yesterday.
Future	I *will play* in a tournament someday.
Present Perfect	He *has played* many different sports. They *have played* together a lot.
Past Perfect	He *had played* golf for hours before noticing his watch was missing.
Future Perfect	Their team *will have played* together for three years.
Present Progressive	I *am playing* with the kids today. You *are playing* so well lately! She *is playing* soccer for the first time.
Past Progressive	He *was playing* with the kids yesterday.
Future Progressive	She *will be playing* professionally one day.
Present Perfect Progressive	I *have been playing* drums for over a year.
Past Perfect Progressive	He *had* not *been playing* poker until we invited him to join our game.
Future Perfect Progressive	I *will have been playing* on this softball team for eight years by the time I take over as manager next spring.

LITTLE HELPER VERBS

You'll notice that many of the verb tenses consist of more than one word. In each case, the last word is the *main verb* and the other word or words are called *helping verbs*. They help express something about the main verb. Let's quickly review how the different tenses are used.

Use the *present* tense to convey the following.

- Present action:

    She <u>dances</u> beautifully.

- Habitual action:

    He <u>practices</u> every day.

- Literary (in the broadest sense) or artistic action:

    In the comics, Dagwood Bumstead <u>begs</u> Blondie for food every time she cooks.

    King Lear <u>is</u> already old when the play <u>begins</u>.

    Chagall's characters <u>float</u> in midair in his paintings.

- Timeless or universally accepted truths:

    Galileo discovered that the earth <u>revolves</u> around the sun.

    A bird in the hand <u>is</u> worth two in the bush.

Use the *present perfect* tense to convey the following.

- An action that started in the past and is still going on:

    I <u>have lived</u> in this apartment eight years. [. . . and I'm still here]

- An action that has been completed but is somehow still connected to the present:

  I have bought a house on your block. [. . . and will now be living there]

  He has drunk too much wine. [and now has a headache]

  The Yankees have won the World Series! [they have just won it, recently]

Use the *past* tense to convey a completely completed action:

  The Yankees won the World Series last year.

  I ate dinner and went to bed.

Use the *past perfect* tense to convey an action already taking place in the past while another past action occurred:

  The Yankees were winning [*past perfect*] when I fell [*past*] asleep.

Use the *future* tense to convey an action that has not yet taken place:

  Stacey will go back to school one day.

  Nancy finishes school next spring. [The present tense *finishes* functions in the future tense as a result of its context (*next spring*), which is perfectly acceptable.]

Use the *future perfect* tense to convey an action that is the past of the future (Whoa!):

  By next year, Ellen will have written her third novel.

Use all the *progressives* to convey a continuous or perpetual action taking place within any other tense:

> Lisa is studying economics.
>
> Tom has been praying for rain
>
> In September, Doug will have been painting for twenty years.

Be Consistent in the Tenses You Use

Unless you are trying to show actions that happen at different times, keep your verbs in the same tense. Check out the following examples:

- When Marco *left* work, he *was* exhausted. (OKAY—both verbs are past tense)
- When Marco *leaves* work, he *is* exhausted. (OKAY—both verbs are present tense)
- When Marco *left* work, he *is* exhausted. (NOT OKAY—don't switch verb tenses for actions that happen at the same time)

Here are some trickier examples:

- Carrie *will go* [future] to college if she *finds* [present] the money for tuition. This is okay because the future action *will go* depends on the present action *finds*. They are not happening at the same time.
- Rocio *had been living* [past progressive] in Bogota for ten years when she decided [simple past] to leave. This is also okay because the first action had already been going on for a time when the second action takes place.

Before You Tense Up

English has many regular verbs that follow predictable rules as they change tenses. However, to keep things interesting, English also has many verbs that are "irregular." (*To talk* is a regular verb. *To write* is an irregular verb.) You do not need to stop and memorize the principal parts of all irregular verbs, but you should familiarize yourself with the list in Appendix C. We include many common irregular verbs, but a good dictionary lists the three principal parts of all of them; don't hesitate to use your dictionary as a reference.

	REGULAR VERB	IRREGULAR VERB
Present	talk	write
Past	talked	wrote
Past Participle	talked	written

There is also the *present participle*, but this is always the -*ing* or gerund form of the verb (*talking, writing*), so we don't include it. These terms will make sense if you look back over the examples of all twelve tenses.

To Conjugate Tricky Irregular Verbs. Some irregular verbs, such as *lie* and *lay*, can be very confusing. Not only are their conjugations tricky, their meanings are easily confused. When in doubt, always look up confusing verbs in a dictionary or grammar reference book. But what if a question comes up when you have no references nearby? Try the following:

- Improvise! Substitute another verb that you are clear about.
- Rewrite the sentence or change the tense.

Do whatever works to express yourself clearly and accurately; it's no crime to avoid a difficult or confusing word. Just make sure the one you substitute is equally appropriate. Here are some examples.

I (*lay* or *laid?*) the baby in his crib.

I *put* the baby in his crib.

I have been (*lying* or *laying?*) down too much lately.

I have been *napping* too much lately.

He had just (*lain* or *laid?*) his head on the desk for ten minutes.

He had just *rested* his head on the desk for ten minutes.

The answers, if you insist on using the original verbs, are *lay, lying,* and *laid.* Complete conjugations for *lay* and *lie* appear in Appendix C.

Exercise 3

Here's an in-tense verb workout for you. In each of the following sentences, one verb must be changed so that it agrees in tense with the other verbs. Cross out the incorrect verb and write in the correct form.

1. Josephine buys candy every day and eats it during her classes; her classmates don't mind because she shared it with them.

2. When Frances moved to Nova Scotia, she sells her home and invited all her friends to come visit.

3. Don likes to get in his car, turn on the radio, rolled down the windows, and speed off into the blue.

VERBALS

Verbals are words made from verbs, but they do not function as verbs in a sentence. There are three categories of verbals: infinitives, participles, and gerunds.

An *infinitive* consists of *to* plus the base form of the verb.

> "*To be* or not *to be*" was Hamlet's famous dilemma. (infinitive used as subject)
>
> I want *to run* as fast as Michael Johnson. (infinitive used as direct object)

A *participle* is used as a modifier (descriptive word). The present participle ends in *-ing*; the past participle ends in *-ed* or an irregular ending.

> He is a *running* fool. (regular verb, modifies *fool*)
>
> She prefers *worn* furniture. (irregular verb, modifies *furniture*)
>
> He is a *scarred* survivor. (regular verb, modifies *survivor*)

A *gerund* is the *-ing* form of the verb used as a noun.

> *Living* well is the best revenge.
>
> "There's no *crying* in baseball!"

THOSE MOODY VERBS

Verb tenses express three moods: indicative, imperative, and subjunctive. The *indicative mood* is used for statements and questions: I was in charge of the classroom. The imperative mood is used for commands or requests: Please *return* to your seats.

The *subjunctive mood* is used for expressing a wish, a doubt, a supposition, or a condition that does not actually exist. In the subjunctive, use *were* instead of *was*; use *had* instead of *has*, *have*, or *would have*. The subjunctive is passing out of use in American English, but here are a couple of situations in which you still find it being used:

~~~∘ **POWER LINE** ∘~~~

Abraham Lincoln, the sixteenth president of the United States, was a master of the English language. He used the subjunctive correctly (and with brilliant, self-deprecating wit) to deflect a criticism about himself. "If I were two-faced," he asked a critic, "would I be wearing this one?"

> If I *were* [not *was*] in charge, we would not go to war.
>
> She wishes her grandmother *were* [not *was*] still alive.
>
> If I *had thought* [not *would have thought*] things through, I might have agreed.
>
> Suppose he *had come* [not *would have come*] to the party.
>
> He acts as if he *had* [not *has*] all the time in the world.

ACTIVE AND PASSIVE VOICE

After all we've said about the subject of the sentence being the actor, we're now going to confess that there is an exception to this rule. There is a special case in which the subject of a sentence is not the actor but the *receiver* of the action. Read the following sentences:

> Interim markdowns may have been taken.
>
> Everything is being done to ensure passenger safety.
>
> This paper has been recycled.
>
> The families have been notified by the police.

Who is the actor in each of these sentences? *Markdowns, everything, paper,* and *families.* These subjects are not *doing* or *being* anything; they are having an action *done to them.* But by whom? The doer is not even mentioned in the first three sentences. This is what we call the *passive voice;* the actor, instead of acting, is passively being acted upon by an implied actor or by an actor mentioned in a *by* phrase.

> Interim <u>markdowns</u> <u>may have been taken</u> [by the store manager].
>
> <u>Everything</u> <u>is being done</u> [by the pilot] to ensure passenger safety.
>
> This <u>paper</u> <u>has been recycled</u> [by its manufacturer].
>
> The <u>families</u> <u>have been notified</u> [by the police].

Use the *active voice* whenever possible. It is more direct and often paints a clearer picture. On occasion, the passive voice can be useful; for instance, if you really don't know the actual subject, as in "The flowers were left on my doorstep." (*Flowers* is the subject; *were left* is the verb.) But don't use it to avoid responsibility, as so many politicians do: "The tax bill has been signed into law" rather than "I signed the tax bill."

Exercise 4

Circle the correct verb form.

1. There (was, were) two puppies sleeping in the box.

2. I wish he (was, were) better prepared for the exam.

3. Either of the two professors (make, makes) a good mentor in physics.

4. *Dubliners* (are, is) one of the best collections of short stories ever written.

5. The bushel of apples (were, was) delivered on time.

6. The boys and I (am, are) staying late to put up the decorations.

7. Neither the stallion nor the two mares (likes, like) being saddled.

8. In our college, economics (attract, attracts) more students than ever.

9. (Are, Is) *The Simpsons* still your favorite show?

10. His biggest obstacle (was, were) his fears.

11. Yesterday, without warning, one of the pipes in the building (burst, bursted).

12. Evelyn, along with her cousin, (organize, organizes) the music festival every year.

13. Hugh (wrote, had wrote) his wife a letter once a week, whether he was on the road or at home.

14. The reason for my outburst (was, were) the pressures building up at work.

15. If Russell (had, would have) been there, he would have stopped the fight.

CHAPTER FOUR

We're on the Case: In Search of the Elusive Pronoun

Read this sentence out loud:

> When Mimi went to Mimi's room for the night, Mimi said goodnight to Mimi's parents and told Mimi's parents to have a good time, as Mimi's parents were staying up late to watch Mimi's parents' favorite show on Mimi's parents' new television set.

Under no circumstances would you ever write such a sentence! But what is so wrong with it? It's repetitive; it's awkward; it's boring. Why? Because no pronouns are used. Look how pronouns completely change the sentence:

> When Mimi went to *her* room for the night, *she* said good night to *her* parents and told *them* to have a good time, as *they* were staying up late to watch *their* favorite show on *their* new television set.

Plug In

See how much pronoun power you already have by tackling this opening quiz. In each of the following sentences, circle the correct pronoun.

1. Fred whispered to his wife, "Let's keep this a secret between you and (I, me)."

2. (We, Us) students began our adventure at dawn.

3. Charlayne and (I, myself) are handling all the renovations.

4. He is one of those doctors (who, whom) others frequently ask for advice.

5. Steven and I are both hearty eaters, but Steven can eat more than (I, me).

6. Each of the books is in (its, their) proper place on the shelves.

7. Dotty gave a party for Bob and (I, me).

WHAT IS A PRONOUN?

Any serious theatrical production, whether it's staged on Broadway, in a regional playhouse, or at a local high school, has stand-ins available for those moments when the stars themselves can't go on. Sentences—minidramas that they are—also depend on stand-ins; in fact, they use them all the time, not just because the star is ailing (words are amazingly resilient), but for variety, clarity, and ease of communication. *Pronouns* are these noun stand-ins. The word a pronoun replaces is called the *antecedent* ("that which goes before").

Pronouns are unassuming little words. You rarely notice them until you accidentally send the wrong one onto the stage. Then it stands alone in the glare of the spotlight, naked and embarrassed. However, if you pay attention to a handful of "red light" situations— situations where you need to put your foot on the brake and pause for a moment—you can usually avoid exposing the wrong pronoun to the public.

To Correctly Use Pronouns. Everything you need to know about pronouns can be summed up in one general rule: Pronouns must be properly matched to the words they stand for. The entire chapter simply elaborates on this rule.

IN CASE YOU'RE INTERESTED . . .

To talk about pronouns, we need to mention one of those grammatical terms that probably gave you the willies when you were in school: case. It's not a big deal. Honest. In chapter 2, we discussed the different roles that nouns could play in your sentences. (If you skipped this section, you might want to take a quick look at the material.)

Since pronouns have to stand in for nouns, they can do whatever nouns can do. The difference is, pronouns change their form to reflect the role they are playing; nouns don't. So when pronouns act as subjects they have one form, when they act as objects they have another form, and when they act as possessors (owners) of something, they have yet another form. These different forms are called case. Here is how the cases look, and the roles pronouns play:

PRONOUN CASE CHART

Subjects	Objects	Possessors
I, we (1st person)	me, us (1st person)	my, our (1st person)
you (2nd person)	you (2nd person)	your (2nd person)
he, she, it, they (3rd person)	him, her, it, them (3rd person)	his, her, its, their (3rd person)

COMPOUND STRUCTURES

The following situations are the most likely to cause problems involving case when you have compound structures.

To Choose the Correct Pronoun Case with Compound Structures. When you have a compound subject or object, ignore the first noun or pronoun, and see which case fits the remaining pronoun.

Bill and I went to the movie. (*Bill* and *I* is a compound; ignore *Bill*)

Correct: *I* went to the movie.

Wrong: *Me* went to the movie.

Her and I went to the movies. (*Her* and *I* is a compound; ignore *Her*)

Correct: *I* went to the movies.

But, in the last example, since *I* is the subject form of the pronoun, and both pronouns in a compound structure have to be the same case, you also need to change *her*. The subject form of *her* is *she*. The correct sentence reads:

Correct: *She and I* went to the movies.

Here's how the "Ignore the First Noun or Pronoun to See which Case Fits the Remaining Pronoun" rule works with some compound object examples:

Tami met *Spencer and I* at the movie. (*Spencer and I* is a compound; ignore *Spencer*)

Wrong: Tami met *I* at the movie.

Tami met *Spencer and me* at the movie. (*Spencer* and *me* is a compound; ignore *Spencer*)

Correct: Tami met *me* at the movie.

Correct: Tami met *him and me* at the movie.

You know from the previous sentence that *me* is correct; therefore, the other pronoun in the compound must also be in the object case. *Him* is the object case; therefore the last sentence above is correct.

Your ear for the correct pronoun is an excellent tool; it gets confused only when it hears a compound structure! If you apply this test, you will *never* make a mistake when using pronouns as part of a compound.

To Choose the Correct Pronoun Case (The Cheating Method). If you're having trouble selecting the correct pronoun, copy the "Pronoun Case Chart" (from the previous page) onto a notecard, or tear it out of the book and tape it over your desk. (Hey, you paid for the book; you can do whatever you want with it!) That way, when you go to apply the pronoun rules, you can easily see which case you need.

To Choose the Correct Pronoun Case After Forms of the Verb *To Be*. First, we'll tell you the "official" rule:

- After all forms of the linking verb *to be*, use a subject pronoun. (See chapter 3 if you've forgotten what a linking verb is.)

It was *I*.

It is *we*.

That can't be *she*.

It might have been *they*.

When the bell rings, it will be *he*.

That's the rule. And, we have to admit, it's logical. By definition, a noun or pronoun that follows a linking verb restates the subject of the sentence; therefore, pronouns used in this way must be in the subject form.

Reality check! The problem is, to most American (as opposed to British) ears, this usage often sounds painfully formal, stilted, and even a trifle snobbish. What to do? Just as the waves of the ocean gradually wear down the rocks on the shore (or, less poetic but closer to home, just as a two-year-old's demands for candy in the grocery store checkout line gradually drive you to abandon all principles and buy the bag of chocolates half an hour before dinner), so does popular usage gradually make a dent in the official rules. Relax. Everybody buys the candy sometimes. As a result, the informal, technically incorrect object form of the pronoun has become acceptable in many situations. Fido doesn't like it, but he's lost this round. However, in all formal situations—doctoral dissertations, job applications, diplomatic functions, etc.—we throw him a bone and use the subject pronoun. Otherwise, the following examples are now generally acceptable in American English:

Is Evelyn home? Yes, that's *her* asleep on the couch.

Were those your cousins sitting in the balcony? No, that wasn't *them*.

That guy walking down Columbus Avenue looks just like Woody Allen; wait, it is *him!*

Is it just *me*, or do you get confused sometimes too?

- Now, the "real-world" rule. After the *to be* form of the verb, always use the object pronoun:

Who's going to be the new team captain? I would like it to be *me*.

With my luck, the boss will turn out to be *him*.

To Choose the Correct *Who* vs. *Whom* Pronoun Case. To decide which case is called for in a *who/whom* or *whoever/whomever* phrase, try this: Substitute *he* or *him* (or *she* or *her*) into the word grouping and see which sounds correct. Consider this sentence:

> The boy (who/whom) she met lives nearby.

The word group in question is *who/whom she met*. Here are the steps that will lead you to a correct pronoun choice:

1. Reverse the order to make the meaning clear: *she met (who/whom)*.
2. Substitute *he* or *him* for *who* and *whom*: she met *he* or she met *him*. The correct choice is *him*. Therefore choose *whom*.

> The boy *whom* she met lives nearby. (correct)

Here's another example:

> If I had known (who/whom) she was, I would have introduced myself.

The word group in question is *who/whom she was*. Now the two steps:

1. Reverse the order to make the meaning clear: *she was who/whom*.
2. Substitute *she* or *her* for *who/whom*: she was *she* or she was *her*.

Remember the formal rule for conjugated forms of *to be*: Use the subject form of the pronoun. She was *she*. Therefore choose the subject form *who*.

> If I had known *who* she was, I would have introduced myself.

To Use the Correct Pronoun Form Before Gerunds. Use the possessor form of the pronoun before gerunds (for a refresher on *-ing* words used as nouns, see chapter 1).

> She resents *his* (not *him*) playing basketball all day.
>
> He had no patience for *their* (not *them*) whining about homework.
>
> Our parents were proud of *our* (not *us*) running in the marathon.

To Use the Correct Pronoun Form After Prepositions. Always use the object form of the pronoun after prepositions.

> Here is a gift from *me*.
>
> You can go with *her*.
>
> Sit quietly beside *him* on that bench.

This becomes tricky only when there is more than one object. Use the foolproof test explained above under compound structures on page 61: Eliminate the first noun or pronoun and then make your choice. Try this sample sentence:

> Derek is going to the game with (she/her) and (I/me).

Eliminate the first part of the compound:

> Derek is going to the game with (I/me).

Test your choices:

> Derek is going to the game with *I*.
>
> Derek is going to the game with *me*. (correct)

Therefore, both pronouns need to be in the object form:

> Derek is going to the game with *her* and *me*.

To Use the Correct Pronoun Form After *Between*. The single most troublesome preposition in this situation is *between*. If you remember no other rule about pronoun case, remember this: Never use the subject form of a pronoun after *between*.

Use between *you and me*   **Not** between *you and I*

Use between *Peggy and me*   **Not** between *Peggy and I*

Use between *him and me*	**Not** between *he and I* (or *him and I*)
Use between *her and me*	**Not** between *she and I* (or *her and I*)
Use between *them and me*	**Not** between *they and I* (or *them and I*)

To Use the Correct Pronoun Form in Appositive Phrases. When used as appositives (words that restate the noun), pronouns take the same case as the noun they are renaming:

> The two boys, Larry and *he*, are sleeping. (*boys* is the subject, so the pronoun is in the subject case *he*.)

> Daisy saw the two boys, Larry and *him*. (*boys* is the object of the verb *saw*, so the pronoun is in the object case *him*.)

To Use the Correct Pronoun Form in Comparisons. You can figure out whether to use the subject or object case by expanding the sentence and seeing which fits:

> She is funnier than (he/him).

Expand the sentence:

> **Correct:** She is funnier than *he* is.
>
> **Wrong:** She is funnier than *him* is.

Try this example:

> She is taller than (I/me).

Expand the sentence:

> **Correct:** She is taller than *I* am.
>
> **Wrong:** She is taller than *me* am.

But take a look at this example:

> Do you like Professor Danto more than (me/I)?

Expand the sentence:

Correct: Do you like Professor Danto more than *I* [do]?

Also Correct: Do you like Professor Danto more than [you like] *me*?

In examples like this, depending on the context, you may have to write out your expanded sentence to make the meaning clear and unambiguous for your reader.

TEST YOUR REFLEXES

You can recognize *reflexive pronouns* because they all end in *-self* or *-selves*:

myself	himself	itself	yourselves
yourself	herself	ourselves	themselves

A reflexive pronoun is one that refers to itself; therefore, these pronouns can be used to refer only to a noun or pronoun already mentioned in the same sentence.

⌇⌇⌇ **POWER LINE** ⌇⌇⌇
"Allow myself to introduce . . . myself."
—Austin Powers

Emphasis is one use for reflexive pronouns:

> Anthony *himself* returned the money he had stolen.
>
> I *myself* saw nothing strange that night.

Unless you are sure there can be no confusion, place the reflexive pronoun immediately after the noun or pronoun it refers to. This way you can avoid sentences like the following:

Wrong: Are you cooking yourself for Thanksgiving? (Ouch!)

Revised: Are you yourself cooking for Thanksgiving?

Clarity is another use for reflexive pronouns:

Anna told her daughter she was going to buy her a dress. (The daughter is getting a new dress.)

Anna told her daughter she was going to buy *herself* a dress. (Anna is getting the new dress.)

⌇ᴡᴠᴠ **POWER LINE** ᴠᴠᴡ⌇

"Today, I consider myself the luckiest man on the face of the earth."

—former New York Yankee Lou Gehrig

You can also use reflexive pronouns when your subject does something to itself, or feels something about itself:

She promotes *herself* constantly.

Do not substitute reflexive pronouns for subject or object pronouns.

Wrong: Phillip and *myself* are getting a divorce. (*Myself* does not refer to a word already used in the sentence, so don't use it. Use *I.*)

Correct: Phillip and *I* are getting a divorce.

Wrong: Leave a message for *myself* on the answering machine. (*Myself* does not refer to another word in this sentence, so don't use it. Use *me.*)

Correct: Leave a message for *me* on the answering machine.

KAPLAN

Exercise 1

If the italicized pronoun is correct, write "C" in the space. If it is wrong, write in the correct pronoun.

1. _____ The teacher and *myself* organized a reading of the play.

2. _____ The caterers left the decision up to Nicholas and *herself*.

3. _____ I *myself* supervised the renovations.

4. _____ This was a task best handled by *ourselves*.

5. _____ The students *themselves* designed the physics course.

PRONOUN REFERENCE

If the noun that a pronoun replaces (the antecedent) is absent, ambiguous, vague, or unclear in any way, you have a problem with faulty reference and need to rewrite your sentence. Check out the following weak sentences and their stronger rewrites.

Grammar Bloopers

• Misuse of the reflexive pronoun made this classified housecleaning ad much more intriguing: "Tired of cleaning yourself? Let me do it."

• There's something wrong with the pronoun reference in this newspaper headline: "TWO SOVIET SHIPS COLLIDE, ONE DIES"

Absent: In France, *they* know a lot about wine in France. (Who is *they*?)
Rewrite: French people know a lot about wine.

Absent: *It* tells about the Civil War in this book. (What does *it* refer to?)
Rewrite: This book tells about the Civil War.

Unclear:	Madeleine told Shauna that *she* had just been chosen for the team. (Who made the team?)
Rewrite:	When Madeleine was chosen for the team, she told Shauna. (Madeleine made the team.)
Rewrite:	Madeleine congratulated Shauna on being chosen for the team. (Shauna made the team.)

Vague:	I'm going to take up basketball. *They* make good money. (Basketballs don't make money; players do.)
Rewrite:	I'm going to become a basketball player. *They* make good money.

Vague:	Although Arnie had never jumped out of a plane before, he was not afraid of *it*. (Not afraid of what? The plane? No. Not afraid of jumping? Yes—but the word *jumping* doesn't appear as an antecedent.)
Rewrite:	Although Arnie had never jumped out of a plane before, he was not afraid.

Vague:	When your kids reach a certain age, you must prepare to talk to them about sex, even if you've never done *it* before. (Hmmm; you figure out what's wrong with this one and how to rewrite it!)

PERSON AND NUMBER CONSISTENCY

When you use pronouns, don't switch from person (*I, you, he, she, they*, etc.) to person in your writing. Try to be consistent.

Wrong:	When a *hiker* sets out on the trail, *you* should have plenty of supplies.
Correct:	When *you* set out on the trail, *you* should have plenty of supplies.

Correct: When a *hiker* sets out on the trail, *he or she* should have plenty of supplies.

Wrong: *One* should be considerate when speaking to *your* parents.

Correct: *One* should be considerate when speaking to *one's* parents.

Correct: *You* should be considerate when speaking to *your* parents.

Here's another pronoun consistency issue: Don't switch from singular to plural. Here is a classic example.

Wrong: One should be considerate when speaking to *their* parents.

Correct: One should be considerate when speaking to *one's* parents.

SEX AND THE SINGLE PRONOUN

Sex is always a touchy subject, but it had to come up sometime. Getting your mind out of the gutter, we're really talking about gender agreement (and number, too). Here's the rule of thumb: Pronouns should agree with their antecedent in gender and number.

A specific gender is easy:

The boy went to *his* room.

That lady dropped her change; *she* will miss the bus.

Plurals are also easy:

The fans rooted for *their* (not *his*, *her*, or *its*) team.

But it's not always clear in some cases regarding gender and number. What about the following sentences?

Each human being strives to do *his* best.

Everyone has *his* own opinion on the subject.

After a student finishes the exam, *he* should turn it in to the teacher.

These sentences are, technically speaking, grammatically correct. But they are troubling to many people. Can you see why?

When an antecedent is *singular* (*each human being, everyone, a student*) but includes *both sexes*, what do you do? Substituting a male pronoun to stand for all people was generally accepted for many years, but this usage came under attack in the late '60s and early '70s. After all, women make up slightly more than half of the world's population; many of them, understandably, were not happy with a pronoun usage that rendered them invisible. Here are some corrections that became popular for awhile:

Each human being strives to do *his or her* best.

Everyone has *his/her* own opinion on the subject.

After a student finishes the exam, *s/he* should turn it in to the teacher.

The first solution works fine for an individual sentence, but if you keep repeating *his or her* or *he or she* throughout a letter, memo, paper, or discussion, the phrase becomes tedious.

The other two solutions are just plain awful. Why? Because they are not only awkward, they are also artificial. There is no such creature as a *s/he*, or a *him/her*, so when you read these terms, your first response is to think of a cold grammatical construct rather than a human being. This dehumanizes your writing. Yes, we know that in certain academic and business circles such writing is not only acceptable, it's considered normal, but we're ready to storm the barricades over this one. (You'll notice we avoided saying, "We're ready to man the barricades . . . .")

Fortunately, there are many creative solutions to the problem of sex and the single pronoun. Here are our favorites.

Replace pronouns with articles. In the following example, notice how using *a* saves the gender day.

Problematic:	Before the audition, each actor must submit *his or her* photograph.
Better:	Before the audition, each actor must submit a photograph. (It's obvious the producers don't want a picture of the family dog.)

Use plurals in place of singular forms. When it comes to being "more correct" with pronouns and the gender issue, there's safety in numbers.

Problematic:	Each doctor felt rewarded for *his* participation in the clinic.
Better:	The doctors felt rewarded for their participation in the clinic.

Delete the pronoun(s) entirely. Your mother was right: When in doubt, leave it out.

Problematic:	The student can depend on peer tutors to help solve *his/her* writing problems.
Better:	The student can depend on peer tutors to help solve writing problems.

Use a *who* phrase to avoid a personal pronoun. It's a bit awkward and convoluted, but it beats being sexist!

Problematic:	If a motorist calls for help, *she* must pay for the call.
Better:	A motorist who calls for help must pay for the call.

Rewrite the sentence to avoid a gender-specific pronoun. Many grammarians have this rule at the top of their hit parade—and it's practical.

Problematic:	Every customer deserves the most courteous service we can give *him*.
Better:	Every customer deserves our most courteous service.

If necessary, repeat the noun. It's not a very elegant solution, but repetition can totally clarify your sentence.

| Problematic: | Always do your best for the patient, no matter how cranky s/he is. |
| Better: | Always do your best for the patient, no matter how cranky the patient is. |

Whether you're aware of it or not, your choice of pronouns in these situations reflects a position on the subject of the equality of the sexes. You can use a singular male pronoun or a singular female pronoun when making general statements, or you can write in such a way that you include both sexes. All these alternatives can be grammatically correct. Whatever you choose, do it consciously, so that your words are a genuine reflection of your beliefs.

Exercise 2

In each of the following sentences, circle the correct pronoun(s).

1. The victim of the practical joke turned out to be (I, me).

2. We objected to (him, his) taking all the credit.

3. (We, Us) managers must assume a leadership role.

4. Norman and (myself, I) are cousins.

5. The play could never have been produced without (he and I, him and me).

6. One has to work hard to build up (your, one's) muscles.

7. What can we do to stop (them, their) worrying about us?

8. The defeat did not hurt him so much as (they, them).

9. They notified everyone except Margie and (she, her).

10. For (who, whom) was the gift intended?

Which Witch is Which? Using Modifiers to Describe, Distinguish, and Explain

The contributions of modifying words and phrases are enormous. They add detail, color, specificity, and clarity to the stories we tell. They distinguish one player from another in the drama of our sentences. They show us how and where and when things happen. Such words are called adjectives and adverbs.

Plug In

In this exercise, certain modifiers (adjectives or adverbs) appear in italics. Draw a line to show what word they modify. If the form of the modifier is incorrect, correct it.

1. She learns *quick*.

2. Did he seem *nervous* during the interview?

3. The players were all *real* tired after the game.

4. Sit there *quiet* until I come get you.

5. Carolyn did *well* on her exam.

6. He is the least *likeliest* person to go into business.

7. The car runs *good* most of the time.

8. Doesn't Granny look *beautifully* tonight?

AD LIBS: WHO SETS THE STAGE?

Adjectives are like makeup artists, costume designers, sound and lighting technicians of the stage: They shape what we see or hear about the actors who appear on stage, so that the images we get become more precise and, in some cases, more memorable, than they otherwise would have been. Adjectives always modify nouns or pronouns:

> the *tall* man
>
> an *older* woman
>
> that *goofy* guy
>
> the *last* bite
>
> a *happy* ending
>
> the *chestnut* filly
>
> the *secret* me

Adverbs are similar to the stage directions in a play, telling the actors *how* or *where* or *when* to move or speak or act. Adverbs modify verbs, adjectives, and other adverbs:

> The horse ran *swiftly*. (How did the horse run? It ran *swiftly*; *swiftly* modifies the **verb** ran.)
>
> The horse was *very* swift. (How swift was the horse? It was *very* swift; *very* modifies the **adjective** swift.)
>
> The horse ran *very* swiftly. (How swiftly did the horse run? It ran *very* swiftly; *very* modifies the **adverb** *swiftly*, which modifies the verb *ran*.)

Exercise 1

How *swiftly* can you run through the following paces? Modify your stride and decide whether the underlined word is an adjective or an adverb. Write your answer in the space provided. It may be helpful to first draw an arrow from the underlined word to the word it modifies: If that word is a noun, the underlined word must be an adjective. If that word is a verb, adjective, or other adverb, you have an adverb.

1. _____ He dances <u>beautifully</u>.

2. _____ Give her <u>more</u> soup.

3. _____ Are you <u>too</u> tired to come with me?

4. _____ Katie is <u>usually</u> adventurous.

5. _____ I'd like <u>another</u> cup of coffee.

6. _____ I am <u>fully</u> aware of the consequences.

7. _____ He was <u>initially</u> put off by her outspokenness.

8. _____ However, he <u>later</u> admired her for it.

9. _____ He comforted the <u>frightened</u> child.

10. _____ She had some <u>lingering</u> doubts about the relationship.

ADJECTIVES VS. ADVERBS

Round One: Where Does *-ly* Fit In the Ring?

Most adverbs are formed by adding the suffix *-ly* to an adjective.

Your phone is loud. It rings loud*ly*.

She has a voracious appetite for books. She reads voracious*ly*.

Have you ever had an absentminded professor? Such professors absentminded*ly* misplace their papers.

This painting is the real thing. It is real*ly* impressive.

Of course, English being English, there are exceptions:

- A number of adverbs do not end in -ly (*not* itself is one of them). These include: *very, often, seldom, quite, too.*
- On the other hand, some words that do end in -ly are not adverbs but adjectives: *friendly, womanly, silly, frilly, courtly, saintly, nightly, daily.* Don't be fooled by how they look.

> Fido is a *friendly* dog.
>
> He was a *courtly* gentleman.
>
> She continues her *daily* routine.

Round Two: Who Modifies What?

Adjectives are always used to modify nouns. In English, adjectives usually go before the noun.

> They drank the *cool* water.

Adjectives are also often used after a linking verb (check chapter 3 to bone up on your linking verbs).

> The water was *cool*.

Adverbs, on the other hand, are used to modify verbs, adjectives, and other adverbs. In the following sentences, the adverbs (in italics) modify the verbs (underlined twice).

> He *hurriedly* <u>left</u> the room.
>
> We <u>ate</u> *heartily*.
>
> She <u>did</u> *not* <u>show</u> up for the interview.
>
> <u>Don't</u> <u>answer</u> that question until your lawer arrives.

Adverbs are also used to modify adjectives. In the following examples, the adverbs are italicized and the adjectives they are modifying are underlined twice.

We were amazed by such *extremely* talented children.

Liane is *very* smart.

Although *quite* young, he is *unusually* mature.

Grammar Don't #1

Don't use adjectives to modify verbs:

He sure works hard. (wrong)

He surely works hard. (yes!)

Adverbs also modify other adverbs. We know this sounds a bit like doublespeak, but bear with us and we'll show you what we mean. In the following examples, the adverbs being modified are underlined twice and the modifying adverbs are in italics.

He bats *somewhat* awkwardly for a Major League player, but he gets the job done.

Soldiers learn *very* quickly in the trenches.

Grammar Don't #2

Don't use adjectives to modify other adjectives:

He was hurt bad. (wrong)

He was badly hurt. (correct)

Round Three: Who's In the Ring with Verbs?

As we mentioned earlier in this chapter, adjectives go with linking verbs.

She looks *angry*. (adjective)

That dress is *beautiful*. (adjective)

He appears *suspicious*. (adjective)

Am I too *loud*? (adjective)

Grammar Don't #3

Don't use adjectives to modify adverbs:

I can eat considerable more than my brother. (wrong)

I can eat considerably more than my brother. (correct)

Adverbs work out with action verbs, as shown in the following power sprints:

> She <u>lashed out</u> *angrily* at her boss. (adverb)
>
> She <u>dresses</u> *beautifully*. (adverb)
>
> He <u>glanced</u> *suspiciously* over his shoulder. (adverb)
>
> <u>Do</u> you always <u>sing</u> so *loudly* in the shower? (adverb)

To determine if it's an act or a direct link. Remember, adverbs are used with action verbs, and adjectives are used with linking verbs. Some verbs can be both linking verbs and action verbs, depending on how they are used. If you're not sure whether a word is being used as a linking verb or an action verb, substitute a form of the linking verb *seems*. If the new sentence makes sense, the original verb is also a linking verb; if the new sentence doesn't make sense, the original verb is an action verb. Run the test on the following example:

> Anne looked tired.

Substitute *seemed* for the verb *looked*.

> Anne *seemed* tired. (This makes sense.)

Therefore, *looked* is being used as a linking verb and must be modified by an adjective. Use the adjective *tired* rather than the adverb *tiredly*.

Exercise 2

In the following sentences, if the underlined modifier is correct, put a check in the space provided. If incorrect, write the correct form. Remember: the trick is to identify the word being modified before you make your choice.

1. _____ Is the baby behaving well or <u>badly</u>?

2. _____ She is a <u>good</u> leader.

3. _____ They looked <u>loving</u> at each other.

4. _____ Kelly looks <u>angry</u>.

5. _____ Minnie lashed out <u>angry</u> at her brother.

6. _____ Minnie lashed out, <u>angry</u> at her brother.
(Notice that the punctuation in this sentence is different from that of the previous sentence. How does that affect its meaning and the way the modifiers are used?)

7. _____ He plays the piano <u>beautiful</u>.

8. _____ She feels <u>bad</u> about the misunderstanding.

9. _____ I'm <u>real</u> sorry I missed you at the office.

Round Four: More Tricksters

Okay, we're back in the ring, suited up and ready to go. This time, the question is, which punch gets thrown where? We are going to lead you through a few more tricky maneuvers concerning when to use an adverb or an adjective.

The good, the bad, and the well. For being such simple words, *good*, *bad*, and *well* are often used incorrectly. One thing to remember is that *good* is always an adjective:

> Be a *good* boy.
>
> That is a *good* joke.

Well is usually an adverb:

> We work *well* together.

Don't Let the Simple Question "How Are You?" Make You ILL

CORRECT: I feel good. (*good* is an adjective meaning happy, satisfied)

CORRECT: I feel well. (*well* is an adjective meaning healthy)

CORRECT: I feel bad. (*bad* is an adjective meaning unhappy, uncomfortable)

In each of these sentences, *feel* is a linking verb; it needs to be followed by an adjective, not an adverb; therefore, any of the above answers is correct.

Of course, the next time someone asks about your health, you can always just say "Fine." Most people don't really want to know anyway.

It would be incorrect to say: We work *good* together. *Well*—as a good adverb should—describes the verb *work*. Here is another example:

> The big filly runs well.

It would be incorrect to say: The big filly runs *good*. In the above example *well* is an adverb describing the verb *run*.

But just to keep us all on our toes, *well* can also be an adjective:

> The doctor says I am completely well.

In this case, *well* follows the linking verb *am* and modifies the pronoun *I*: therefore, it is an adjective.

Avoid substituting the adverb form when someone asks how you feel about something:

> How do you feel about losing your job?
>
> I feel badly. (wrong)
>
> I feel bad. (correct!)

Badly is an adverb and must modify an action verb; *to feel* is an action verb only when it refers, literally, to the sense of touch. To say "I feel badly" means something is wrong with your fingertips or hands and you cannot properly receive sensations. (Needless to say, you won't be using this sentence very often.)

If you're not sure whether to use *bad* or *badly*, try substituting *sad* or *sadly* and you'll get it right.

How do you feel about moving to the suburbs?

> I feel bad/badly. (Substitute *sad/sadly*)
>
> I feel *sad*. (correct)
>
> I feel sadly. (wrong)

Therefore, choose *bad*.

When to use *real* and *really*. *Real*, the adjective, defines only nouns and pronouns ("real gold," "the real you"). *Really*, the adverb, is used to modify verbs and adjectives. Something might be "really moving," or "really good," but not "real good." That is, unless you want to be a country-western singer; then it's real fine.

Remember, *real* is an adjective:

> Is that a *real* diamond?
>
> I like the *real* you.

Really is an adverb:

> That diamond is *really* beautiful. (NOT *real* beautiful)
>
> He was *really* sweet to me. (NOT *real* sweet)

PLAYING HOUDINI: TURNING VERBS INTO ADJECTIVES

Verbs are versatile. Take the verbs *to bark* and *to run*. You learned in chapter 3 that you could add *-ing* to these and many other verbs to make nouns:

> That *barking* kept me up all night.
>
> *Running* is her deepest passion.

To turn verbs into adjectives with one stroke of the three-letter wand. Voilà! The *-ing* form of the verb (the present participle) can also function as an adjective:

> What can we do about that *barking* dog?
>
> She needs a new pair of *running* shoes.

If the *-ing* form of the verb is used to modify a noun, it's an adjective:

> the *walking* wounded, the *blustering* boss, the *ringing* phone, my *beating* heart, the *fleeing* robbers, the *laughing* girl, the *struggling* couple, the *continuing* saga.

To turn verbs into adjectives with a stroke of the two-letter wand. Take the verb *to frighten*. Add *-ed* and voila! The past participle of the verb is now an adjective.

> He tried to comfort the *frightened* child.

> The *failed* attempt upset her, but it did not defeat her.

If the *-ed* form of the verb is used to modify a noun, it's an adjective: the *confused* neighbors, the *relieved* coach, the *maligned* student, the *underpaid* teacher, the *overworked* housewife, the *limited* choices.

Exercise 3

Embedded in each adjective is a root that relates to one of the professions listed in the second column. Find the root, then draw a line to connect the adjective to the noun it modifies. For example:

the de**ranged** ─── model
the de**posed** ─── dry cleaner
the de**pressed** ─── cowboy

ADJECTIVES	THE PROFESSIONS
the de**scribed**	electrician
the re**trained**	song writer
the de**lighted**	organ donor
the de**composed**	engineer
the dis**heartened**	writer
the de**barked**	symphony conductor
the dis**concerted**	teacher
the de**toured**	travel guide
the de**tested**	tree surgeon
the di**stressed**	hair stylist

COMPARATIVES AND SUPERLATIVES

We don't promote comparing oneself to others; it can often be the least (not the lesser) gratifying thing to do. But, if you're going to do it, you might as well know how to do it in the most (not more) convincing way.

There are two basic ways to form comparatives and superlatives:

1 Add -er and -est to the root word (a modifier, of course); and
2. Use *more* or *most* in front of the modifier.

> Megan is *taller* (comparative) than Teresa, but Angela is the *tallest* (superlative) of the three girls.
>
> Her boyfriend is eleven years *younger* (comparative) than she.

We add -er to form the comparative and -est to form the superlative. This works for most one-syllable adjectives:

smart	smarter	smartest
sweet	sweeter	sweetest
mean	meaner	meanest

This also works for most two-syllable adjectives ending in -y, -er, or -ow:

lucky	luckier	luckiest
clever	cleverer	cleverest
narrow	narrower	narrowest

We use *more* for the comparative and *most* for the superlative with many words. This works for most two-syllable adjectives **not** ending in -y, -er, or -ow:

tasteless	more tasteless	most tasteless

More and *most* are used to modify adjectives of three or more syllables:

beautiful	more beautiful	most beautiful
outrageous	more outrageous	most outrageous

More and *most* are also used to further modify adjectives with *-ing* or *-ed* endings:

exciting	more exciting	most exciting
warped	more warped	most warped

You don't have to be Superman or Superwoman to memorize the following additional rules regarding comparatives and superlatives.

To compare two items. Always use *-er* or *more* when comparing one person, place, or thing to another person, place, or thing.

> He is the *younger* of the two boys. (NOT *youngest* of the two boys)

> She is the *more* intelligent of the two. (NOT *most* intelligent of the two)

Remember?

He's "Faster than a speeding bullet," but "*more* powerful than a locomotive. . . ."

—Jerry Siegel and Joe Shuster, creators of *Superman* for the comics, 1938

Also, when referring to two items, use the terms *former* and *latter*:

> She could travel to France or Spain; she chose the *latter*.

To compare three or more items. Always use *-est* or *most* to modify a person, place, or thing that stands above the crowd. No need for modesty in this department.

> He is the smart*est* of the three brothers.

> She is the *most* ambitious of all the children.

Also, when comparing three or more items, remember to use *first* and *last*.

> She could travel to France, Italy, or Spain; she chose the *last*.

To compare a thing or a person to a group. Use the phrase *any other* or *anyone else* to make the modifying distinction clear.

> She is smarter than anyone in the class.

She is in the class, so she can't be smarter than herself. Therefore, it would be much clearer written in one of the following ways:

> 1. She is smarter than anyone *else* in the class.
> 2. She is the smartest student in the class.

Here's another example of an unclear modifier:

> They are wealthier than any family in the neighborhood.

This could lead one to wonder how they can be wealthier than themselves. This sentence can be fixed in one of two ways:

> 1. They are wealthier than any *other* family in the neighborhood.
> 2. They are the wealthiest family in the neighborhood.

To compare equivalent things. You've heard the expression, "You can't compare apples and oranges." It refers to the practice of comparing two different categories of things, which doesn't make sense. Here's an example of a comparison of nonequivalent things:

> The coffee at Mary Ann's Café is better than Starbucks. (you're comparing a hot beverage to a franchise)

Correctly revised, this would read:

> The coffee at Mary Ann's Café is better than that at Starbucks.

Here are two more examples of comparing apples to oranges:

1. My friends from school are better than work. (you're comparing people to a place of employment)

2. My bedroom in the old house was bigger than the new house. (you're comparing one bedroom to a whole house)

Correctly revised, the above two statements would read:

1. My friends from school are better than those from work.

2. My bedroom in the old house was bigger than the one in the new house.

In each example, a pronoun has been added to complete the comparison: to make the comparison equivalent. You could also repeat the noun: My bedroom in the old house was bigger *than my bedroom in the new house.*

Tricky Adjectives

We feel compelled to warn you about several trickster adjectives. They are tricky because they are so often misused that we cannot rely on our grammar ear to hear the correct usage. For speaking, as always, you have more leeway. But for the big tests, the formal papers, study the following tricksters.

To know when to use *less* and *fewer*. If the items in question can be counted, use the adjective *fewer*. *Less* is used to describe things that cannot be counted.

People can always be counted. Always use *fewer* when talking about people. And remember to count. You'll have less trouble and make fewer mistakes.

Popcorn without butter has *less* fat than popcorn with butter. (fat cannot be counted)

Popcorn without butter has *fewer* grams of fat than popcorn with butter. (grams can be counted)

Less time, *fewer* hours.

Less money, *fewer* dollars.

Less love, *fewer* lovers.

Less cake, *fewer* cookies.

Less water but *fewer* gallons of water, glasses of water, or sips of water.

Less grammar, *fewer* rules.

> ### Common Mistake
>
> The next time you go to the supermarket, look for the sign over the express line. It will read: *TEN ITEMS OR LESS*. It should say *TEN ITEMS OR FEWER*, because items are individual things that can be counted.

To modify or not to modify absolutes. There is a simple rule to apply to absolutes, which are those adjectives that state the ultimate or perfect degree of something: Don't modify them. You can't be *very* unique because *unique* already means "one of a kind." The heavens can't be *vastly infinite* because *infinite* already means "without end." This also goes for such words as *perfect, unanimous, dead*, etc. (These words can be *qualified*, as in "He was *almost* dead when the doctor arrived," but you can't measure them in degrees: "The vote was *very* unanimous.")

Tricky Adverbs: A Hopeful Lesson

Many adverbs are as tricky as the adjectives discussed in previous pages. Again, misuse is widespread—in fact, so widespread that our hearing has become distorted. Read the following sentences. How do they sound to you?

Hopefully, you'll feel better soon.

Hopefully, Josh will receive your letter.

Hopefully, I will get the promotion.

They may sound right, but there is something wrong with these sentences. *Hopefully* means "in a hopeful manner." Substitute that for the adverb and you'll see the problem: I will, in a hopeful manner, get the promotion. That is not what the speaker means. The speaker means, I hope I will get the promotion.

This is an incorrect usage that irritates some people but rolls right off the backs of others. Technically incorrect, it is so widespread, even among highly educated and articulate writers, that it is gaining a foothold in American English. Hopefully, you'll find an alternative!

Exercise 4

In the following sentence, *only* really gets around. Each time it shifts position, the meaning of the sentence changes. See if you can briefly state what each variation means.

1. Only he took the French course. _____

_____

_____

2. He only took the French course. _____

_____

_____

3. He took only the French course. _____

_____

_____

4. He took the only French course. _____

_____

_____

5. He took the French-only course. _____

_____

_____

YOUR SLIP IS SHOWING: FAULTY MODIFIERS

We can get into trouble when we start using whole phrases rather than single words as our modifiers. The trouble stems from placing these phrases incorrectly. The rule is easy, but the applications can get tricky, and that's why intentional faulty modifiers have always been a staple of comedy.

The rule to remember is this: *Place the modifier as close as possible to the word it modifies.* We often fail to do this primarily by using dangling modifiers, misplaced modifiers and two-way modifiers.

> ∼◇◇◇ **POWER LINE** ◇◇◇∼
>
> "This morning I shot an elephant in my pajamas. How he got into my pajamas I'll never know."
>
> —Groucho Marx, from the movie *Coconuts*

To identify a dangling modifier.
Sometimes words or phrases get attached to the wrong noun because the right noun is missing from the sentence.

> *Upon entering the room*, the picture fell off the wall.

Who or what is entering the room? If one has an active imagination, it could be a number of things. The sentence can be clarified in one of two ways:

1. Upon entering the room, we saw the picture fall off the wall.

2. As we entered the room, the picture fell off the wall. (The modifying phrase is now a clause.)

Here's another example:

> *To teach school effectively*, respect for the students is essential.

Who or what is going to teach school effectively? These dangling modifiers leave a lot to the imagination. The statement can be fixed in one of two ways:

1. To teach school effectively, you must have respect for the students.

2. For you to teach school effectively, respect for the students is essential.

POWER LINE

From the classified section:
Wanted. Man to take care of cow that does not smoke or drink.

To identify misplaced modifiers. In these cases, the modifier is attached to the wrong noun, even though the correct noun is present in the sentence.

I saw the book on the desk that I had borrowed from the library.

Did the speaker really borrow a desk from the library? Probably not. So here's the corrected form:

I saw the book that I had borrowed from the library on the desk.

To identify two-way modifiers. Sometimes a modifier can attach itself to a word shortly before it or to a word shortly after it.

Nonya said *during the meeting* Martha acted like a fool.

What happened *during the meeting*? Did Nonya talk about Martha's behavior? Or did Martha act like a fool? In other words, does the phrase modify *said* or *acted*? Depending on the meaning intended by the writer, this could be rewritten in one of two ways:

1. During the meeting, Nonya said Martha acted like a fool.

2. Nonya said Martha acted like a fool during the meeting.

Exercise 5

Okay. Your modifying muscles have been warmed up, so here's a workout for you. Find and correct the faulty modifiers in the following sentences.

1. Susanna said the book she had been reading quickly bored her to distraction.

2. Rushing to the theater, my heel caught in the sidewalk and broke.

3. To drive a tractor, your patience must match your skill.

4. I was very skeptical when she stated blithely that she almost reads an entire novel in one sitting.

5. To get into the good graces of management, your ability and loyalty must be evident and unquestionable.

6. When viewing it through a veil of smog, the tourist brochure emphasized that Los Angeles is very impressive.

7. Even the students who work hard occasionally do poorly in a testing situation.

8. While standing on station platforms, high-speed trains might pass in either direction at any time.

9. We saw many deer driving through the back roads.

10. At the age of five, my grandmother told me about her escape from Chile to the United States.

11. Hanging awkwardly on the wall above the sofa, Jeremy could not keep his eyes off the new painting in his wife's office.

THE ADVERBIAL SPLIT INFINITIVE: A CHANGING RULE

Remember, an infinitive is a verb with *to* in front of it. A *split infinitive* is when another word is placed between *to* and the verb. The general rule says not to split an infinitive for any reason. The reason for this has been that inserting an adverb into the infinitive often sounds awkward.

Awkward: He told me *to not call* after nine.

Better: He told me *not to call* after nine.

Sometimes, it's not only okay to split an infinitive, it's preferable. Certain combinations of adverbs and verbs have become so closely linked in our consciousness that we want to hear them together:

He began *verbally* to abuse her.

Famous Split Infinitive

Gene Roddenberry's stated mission for the Starship Enterprise was "*to* boldly *go* where no man has gone before." The *Star Trek* television series premiered in 1966, but by the time *Star Trek: The Next Generation* appeared, this line was altered to reflect a changing consciousness about sexism in language. Now the mission is "to boldly go where no one has gone before."

This is technically correct. However, *verbal abuse* is a phrase that we are used to hearing without any intervening words. A better choice for this sentence is:

He began to *verbally abuse* her.

Here's another example:

The bulb was used to inseminate cows artificially.

Technically correct, but we want to emphasize the technique known as artificial insemination. Therefore, we don't want to break it up; it's better to say:

The bulb was used to *artificially inseminate* cows.

The Top Ten Adverbs Used to Split Infinitives*

All of the following adverbs share the same function: they intensify, emphasize, or focus attention on the verb stem, which is where the meaning comes from. That's why people keep breaking the rule. Here's the countdown:

10. ever
 9. completely
 8. finally
 7. even
 6. fully
 5. further
 4. not
 3. actually
 2. just

Here's the drum roll . . . And the number-one adverb used to split infinitives:

 1. really

 **SPARK**

Franklin Roosevelt is reputed to have told his wife Eleanor that he wasn't sure if he should try to run for president of the United States because he was afraid he might fail.

"Well, then, don't," she said.

"Don't try?" he asked.

"No," she answered, "don't fail."

In general, if your meaning is helped or made more precise by splitting the infinitive, do so. If there's no reason for doing so . . . don't.

I want to *really* get to know you. Compare this to: I *really* want to get to know you. The first emphasizes the act of knowing; the second emphasizes the desire. Here are a few more examples of well-chosen split infinitives:

> His only problem was getting the bargain car *to actually work*.

> It's outrageous *to even think* of such a thing at a time like this.

> The therapist hopes *to fully understand* herself, but knows this is impossible.

As you can see, people split infinitives *to really emphasize* their meaning.

*according to COBUILD/Bank of English

Exercise 6

In the following sentences, a modifier has been italicized. 1. Underline the word it modifies; 2. Identify the modifier as an adverb or adjective (the modifier may be a phrase); and 3. If the modifier is correct, write "c"; if incorrect, correct it.

> Example: He threw a wild punch and *unexpectedly* hit his staggering opponent.
>
> ***Unexpectedly*** modifies the verb *hit*; **adverb, correct**

1. He threw a wild punch and unexpectedly hit his *staggering* opponent.

2. Dolores bakes *real* good apple pies.

3. Dolores bakes real *good* apple pies.

4. Gary bakes *well* also.

5. *Grazing on the hillside*, I noticed a herd of sheep.

6. We have *less* students in day classes than in night classes.

7. *At the age of six*, my father took me to my first baseball game.

8. *While I was chatting on the phone*, the bathtub overflowed.

KAPLAN

Punctuation and Other Vital Issues: From Capital-ism to Colon-ialism

You may think the Russian short-story writer Isaac Babel is going a bit too far, but anyone who takes writing seriously comes to appreciate—to one degree or another—the value of precise punctuation. Once you learn the basic punctuation marks, you can use

> ∿ **POWER LINE** ∿
>
> "No iron can pierce the heart with such force as a period put just at the right place."
>
> —Isaac Babel

them to convey all the stops, starts, asides, meanings, and emphases that could be conveyed to a person sitting right across from you.

Punctuation is *practical* insofar as it helps ensure clarity in written communication. Without it, you could easily become lost in a forest of words. With it, you have a symbolic set of guideposts every step of the way, whether you are traveling through a classified ad, an annual report, a poem, or a term paper.

However, punctuation is *stylistic* insofar as it reflects the individual writer's tone and attitude. This is possible because, although there are certain fairly rigid rules governing the use of punctuation marks, there are also situations in which you get to (have to) make your own choices. Different choices can express subtle differences in the writer's approach, so you, the writer, can make decisions based on your own personal goals.

Good writing usually depends on a combination of the clarity that comes from following the rules and the flair that arises from occasionally breaking or bending them—not randomly, but for a purpose.

In this chapter we'll go over the most widely used punctation marks and their most common—and confusing—applications.

Plug In

About the power of punctuation . . . how much do you already know? Punctuate the following sentences, but don't change or rearrange any of the words. Each example should be kept as only one sentence.

1. suzanne visited India Pakistan and Nepal Kelly however visited only India

    _____

2. id be glad to manage your campaign said Rhonda but Ive never done anything that amibitious before

    _____

3. would anyone including you children like to help me out onstage

    _____

4. although its an unusual request the students representative would like to address the faculty next monday at 230

    _____

5. the baby can have any of the following milk juice bananas or cookies

    _____

NO CONFUSION ALLOWED!

There is only one absolute rule that should never be broken: Your reader must not become confused anywhere along the way. With this in mind, read the following sentence:

We have to finish packing Jason before we start the car.

What's going on here? Are we stuffing poor Jason into a trunk? Or packing a suitcase for our infant son? This sentence suggests one of those two possibilities—hopefully (yes, *hopefully*; see chapter 5 if you think we're using this word incorrectly), the latter. However, if we are speaking *to* Jason about our travel plans, we need to add some punctuation to clarify our meaning.

We have to finish packing, Jason, before we start the car.

Now we have a clear and unambiguous sentence, thanks to those two little commas.

Here's another sentence that could have multiple meanings if punctuation is not used to clarify the drama of the sentence:

The coach chose Sally and Latisha and Paula left.

Which of the three women were chosen? Who left? It depends on how you punctuate the sentence. Each of the following sentences, depending on comma placement, conveys a drama quite different from the other.

The coach chose Sally, and Latisha and Paula left.

The coach chose Sally and Latisha, and Paula left.

Placement of the comma is an example of punctuation power: Its small, brief mark upon the page can completely change the meaning of a sentence.

POWER MARKS UPON THE PAGE

The rest of this chapter defines and examines the correct use of the following forms of punctuation: period, question mark, exclamation mark, semicolon, colon, dash, parentheses, hyphen, apostrophe, quotation marks, and capitalization.

The Period

A period is used to mark the end of a sentence unless that sentence is a question or an exclamation. A period signals a full stop. The word itself is used to signify the end of something. Many of you have heard (or used) this classic American sentence:

> "You're not getting the car—period."

This is an emphatic way of saying that the discussion is over, finished, ended, done. That's exactly what the period means in punctuation.

The period works the same whether the sentence is short or long:

> No.
>
> A stitch in time saves nine.
>
> Writing fiction has developed in me an abiding respect for the unknown in a human lifetime and a sense of where to look for the threads, how to follow, how to connect, to find in the thick of the tangle what clear line persists.
>
> (from *One Writer's Life*, by Eudora Welty)

The Question Mark

> Would you like to have dinner with me sometime?
>
> Do I know you?
>
> Are we there yet?
>
> Is this going to be on the test?
>
> What did Nixon know, and when did he know it?

The ability to ask questions is the sign of an intelligent, inquiring mind. The ability to convey a question on paper rests solely on the use of the question mark. It always goes at the end of a complete sentence that is a question. It also follows single word questions and sentence fragments that are questions. The question mark conveys the questioning intonation you would use if you were speaking aloud to someone.

Really?

Why?

Is that right?

Rhetorical Questions are questions to which the speaker doesn't really expect an answer. They are asked for dramatic, sarcastic, or comedic effect.

Dramatic: "If you prick us, do we not bleed?" (Shylock, in *The Merchant of Venice* by William Shakespeare)

Sarcastic: "Did you ever wonder why. . . ?" (Andy Rooney's trademark question on *60 Minutes*.)

Comedic: Why are there locks on the doors of a convenience store that is open 24 hours a day, 365 days a year?
Why are there Interstate Highways in Hawaii?
Why do hot dogs come ten to a package and hot dog buns only eight?
Why do they put Braille dots on the keypad of the drive-up ATM?

The Exclamation Point

An exclamation point follows an expression of great surprise, emphasis, or emotion.

You will probably never need exclamation points in anything you write for work or school. If you do need to express a strong emotion, try to do it through your words. There is

 **SPARK**

If you use the exclamation mark too often, its effect is weakened. Also, you look silly. William Maxwell, an editor at *The New Yorker*, has said (only half-jokingly?) that "a writer gets two exclamation points in a lifetime." A slight exaggeration, perhaps, but you get the idea.

less chance of your being misunderstood. A memo that reads, "I am waiting for your report!" can be interpreted as an angry demand when you intended it as encouragement. If you write, "I am eagerly awaiting your report," your intention is unambiguous. That is, unless you have a reputation for sarcasm. Likewise, if you write, "I am awaiting your report, which was due three days ago," your displeasure is clear; you don't need to emphasize it with an exclamation point, which might seem like childish foot stamping.

However, in personal correspondence, informal, or humorous writing, you will probably use the exclamation point more frequently.

> I can't believe I got such a big raise!
>
> Get out of the street this instant!
>
> Wow!
>
> Ouch!
>
> @#+>?/@ ^ * @=##!

The Comma

The comma may be the most frequently used (and misused) punctuation mark. In general, it indicates a pause in the flow of words or thoughts. Here are its most common uses.

1. **Use a comma to separate two complete thoughts (independent clauses) joined by**

> for
>
> and
>
> nor
>
> but
>
> or
>
> yet
>
> so

The first letter of each of these words forms the acronym FANBOYS, which will help you remember the seven coordinating conjunctions. It may also help to just think of them as "joining" words.

> Ari always goes to Maine for his vacations, but Nancy goes someplace different every year.

> I can stop by to help you with the assignment this evening, or I can come over for a few hours during the weekend.

The comma always goes *before* the joining word.

Just because you see a FANBOY doesn't mean you need a comma before it. FANBOYS have other uses in addition to joining independent clauses.

> *Payton and Cooper* are twins.

> Who is funnier: *Danny or Richard?*

> She *runs faster and jumps higher* than the boys in her class.

> She is *gone but not forgotten*.

> He emerged from the affair *sadder but wiser*.

> It's neither *fish nor fowl*.

When two independent clauses are quite short, some people prefer to leave out the comma.

> Bruce drinks red wine but Betty drinks only white.

However, if you choose to keep the comma in such a sentence, that's fine, too.

> One sings, and the other dances.

> One sings and the other dances.

Like singing and dancing, it's a question of style.

2. **Use a comma to set off *parenthetical* openers or closers.** Parenthetical refers to words, phrases, or clauses that are not essential to the meaning of the sentence.

> *When he looked in the mirror,* Ernie decided he needed a haircut.
>
> *After waiting half an hour,* Mandy left.
>
> The picnic is scheduled for next Sunday, *weather permitting.*
>
> *Furious,* Karen refused to enter the room.

3. **Use commas to set off *parenthetical* insertions** (words, phrases, or clauses inserted into the middle of a sentence—sometimes called "interrupters"). Like openers and closers (see above), insertions add information but are not essential to the meaning of the sentence.

> The motorcycle, *gleaming in the sun,* was the first thing he had ever wanted to own.
>
> Albany, *which is the capital of New York,* is located in the eastern part of the state.

You can tell if a group of words is nonessential by removing it and seeing if the sentence still makes sense.

> The motorcycle was the first thing he had ever wanted to own.
>
> Albany is located in the eastern part of the state.

Yes, they still make sense. But what about this next sentence?

> The woman *who runs the fastest* wins the race.

Should we put commas around this insertion or not? Apply the test:

> The woman wins the race.

Which woman? The information we needed to identify the woman is now missing. When information is necessary to distinguish or identify a noun, it is not set off by commas. That tells us we can't remove it without doing harm to the sentence. Here's another example:

> The students who drop out of school have a harder time.

Which students have a harder time? The students who *drop out of school*. This clause is essential to the meaning of the sentence. You can't remove it, so don't set it off with commas.

Let's take a look at the next two sentences:

> The students, *who were all very tired,* began to fall asleep in class.

> The students *who were tired* began to fall asleep in class.

In the first sentence, if *all* the students were tired, this first clause doesn't limit or distinguish the noun *students*; it merely adds information. Therefore, use commas to indicate that it can be removed. But in the second sentence, not all students fell asleep—only those *who were tired*. This is an important distinction that is essential to the meaning of the sentence; therefore, do not use commas to set off this insertion.

POWER LINE

"*Beulah*, peel me a grape."
—Mae West in *I'm No Angel*

"Open the pod bay doors, *HAL*."
—Keir Dullea in *2001: A Space Odyssey*

"Come on, *baby*, light my fire."
—from "Light My Fire," by the Doors

Always use two commas for a parenthetical insertion: one before, one after. This is how you "set it off" or distinguish it from the essential elements of the sentence. One of the most frequent comma mistakes involves using only one comma to indicate an insertion.

> Mr. Busby, that mean old man is waiting for you.

This is fine if you are warning Mr. Busby about someone else. But if you are speaking *about* Mr. Busby, you had better remember to attach the second comma.

> Mr. Busby, that mean old man, is waiting for you.

To remember when to use two commas. Think of the two commas that set off an insertion as handles with which you can lift the words out of the sentence. That's how you signal a reader that those words may be removed. If the words are essential to identify your noun, don't give them any handles; then the reader can't "lift" them out.

4. **Use commas in direct address.** Commas are always used to set off the name of someone who is being spoken to.

5. **Use commas between all items in a series.** A *series* is three or more items. The items can be as brief as a single word or as long as a clause:

> He bought shirts, ties, and shoes.

> She was thoroughly prepared for her law exams, she answered every question brilliantly, and she passed with flying colors on her first try.

We think the final comma in a series is necessary for two reasons:

First, the combination of the comma plus *and* alerts readers to the fact that they are coming to the end of the series (this is especially useful in a long, involved series).

Second, the comma helps avoid confusion when you have one or more compound items in the series. Here's an example:

> My children's favorite foods were peanut butter and jelly, bagels and cream cheese, and pizza.

If you eliminate the final comma, you have a confusing sentence: Do my children like three separate foods: bagels and cream cheese and pizza? Or do they like the combination of bagels, cream cheese, and pizza all rolled together? (Kids have devised stranger combinations: Ever heard of raisins and ketchup?) If you place the comma between *all* items in a series, you will avoid such confusion.

Sometimes, for stylistic purposes (to increase the sense of relentlessness, or for a certain rhythmic effect), you may choose to leave out the *and* (but not the comma!) between the last two items in a series. Earlier in this chapter, in our discussion of the period, we wrote:

> **Punctuating a Series**
>
> This is one of the rules about which there is much disagreement. Reputable publications such as the *New York Times* do NOT use the final comma before the *and* in a series.

This means the discussion is over, finished, ended, done.

We left out the *and* on purpose to emphasize the blunt finality with which we were concluding our discussion of the period.

How's that for creativity?

6. **Use commas with multiple adjectives.** When you have two or more adjectives before a noun, separate them by commas if each adjective by itself is intended to modify the noun. You can usually test this by joining the adjectives with *and*; if the sentence sounds natural, use a comma.

> We made our way down the *long, winding* road. (the long *and* winding road)
>
> She was a *funny, intelligent* woman. (the funny *and* intelligent woman)

In both cases, these words function as independent adjectives. Therefore, use a comma between them. However, if the first adjective modifies the idea expressed by the combination of the second adjective plus the noun, then don't separate the adjectives by a comma.

> Marly stared at him with icy green eyes.
>
> Marly stared at him with icy *and* green eyes. (awkward)

Icy is really modifying the combination *green eyes*, so you don't need a comma. Here's a similar example:

> Tom was researching neglected tribal customs.
>
> Tom was researching neglected *and* tribal customs. (awkward)

Not only does the second sentence sound awkward, but it could also be misleading, as though Tom were studying two different categories of customs: those that were neglected and those that were tribal. Tom is studying only those *tribal customs* that are also *neglected*; therefore, no comma.

As you can see by how many pages we've devoted to it, the comma is a complicated little thing with many and diverse uses. We're finally ready to travel on to the next punctuation mark.

The Semicolon

The semicolon is used in two main ways:

1. **Use a semicolon to separate two closely related, independent clauses NOT joined by one of the FANBOYS** (*for, and, nor, but, or, yet, so*).

> The girls played basketball; the boys played soccer.

Sometimes, to emphasize a particular relationship between the two clauses, you might add a joining word such as *therefore, furthermore, moreover, however, in addition, on the other hand, consequently, as a result, etcetera*. If you use one of these words or phrases after a semicolon, it needs to be followed by a comma.

> The girls played basketball; *therefore*, the boys played soccer.

> I will not be at work on Friday; *however*, I will drop off the sketches that I promised you.

If these joining words are used for emphasis in the middle of a *single* independent clause, then you treat them as you would any parenthetical insertion and place commas around them.

> She plans, *moreover*, to run for school president.

2. **Use a semicolon to separate items in lists when those items are themselves divided by commas or are very long.**

> We had to buy fruits, vegetables, and whole grains for Reggie; red meat for Sheilah; chips, pretzels, and cookies for Bart; and cheese, yogurt, and ice cream for Lynette.

> We intended to construct multiple units of low-income housing for inner-city tenants; to train the tenants in construction skills during the building phase of the project; to conduct workshops on finance and banking; and to enroll tenants in adult-education classes at various colleges in the neighborhood.

The Colon

(If you master this section, you will have attained the rank of General Colon Power.)

A colon is used after a complete statement to introduce a list, an appositive (a word that renames a noun; chapter 2), an explanation, or a long quotation.

1. **Use a colon to introduce a list.**

> I am going to the store to buy the following: milk, bread, eggs, and coffee.

> We visited four cities in Afghanistan: Herat, Kandahar, Kabul, and Paghman.

Generally, you don't use the colon directly after a verb, because it interrupts the natural flow from verb to object.

> I enjoy: jazz, blues, and classical music.

Why insert this colon? The sentence is smoother without it.

> I enjoy jazz, blues, and classical music.

If you want to use a colon in this sentence, follow the rule and make a complete statement first.

I enjoy music: jazz, blues, and classical.

2. Use a colon to introduce an appositive.

I would like to introduce a truly heroic man: my father.

She had only one dream: to sing on the stage of the Metropolitan Opera.

3. Use a colon to introduce an explanation.

Try this as a method of proofreading: Start with the last sentence of your story and read through one sentence at a time until you reach the beginning.

Here's a suggestion for a quick and easy dinner: buy take-out.

4. Use a colon to introduce a long quotation.

George Orwell has argued: "Political language—and with variations this is true of all political parties, from Conservatives to Anarchists—is designed to make lies sound truthful and murder respectable, and to give an appearance of solidity to pure wind."

A number of situations arise in the business world in which colons are called for (obviously, some of these situations arise outside the office as well).

To use the colon in correspondence. We address business letters to *Whomever*, always followed by a colon, as in the following examples:

Dear Sir or Madam:

Dear Professor Singh:

To use the colon to separate the writer of a letter from the typist. In the bottom left-hand corner of many business letters you'll see:

JSP:ssf

This is the way we signify the writer's initials (JSP in this case) and also acknowledge the typist's role (ssf in this case).

To use the colon regarding copies sent to others. Often a copy of a business letter is sent to others who are involved but to whom the letter is not addressed. The colon is an important part of the following form used to signify to whom copies have been sent:

cc: TRD

bcc: RBW

We realize that carbon copies aren't used anymore, and that most of you have never seen one. These abbreviations are conventions left over from precomputer days and are still accepted, common usage.

To use the colon in memorandums. The memo is frequently used in business and interoffice correspondence. Colons are used to make clear in a brief way whom the memo is to and from, and what it is about.

TO: MMJ	SUBJECT: ACCOUNTS
FROM: BJK	REFERENCE: YOUR PROPOSAL

RE: is commonly used to shorten the reference.

To use the colon in a few other situations. When you have to cite references, use a colon between the volume and page or pages of journals:

Linguistic Inquiry 3:197–209

The colon is also used between the city and publisher in footnotes:

[4]Toni Morrison, *Beloved* (New York: Plume, 1988), p. 139.

The colon is also used to separate the city from the publisher in bibliographies:

Mulisch, Harry. *The Assault*. New York: Pantheon Books, 1985.

The colon is used to make the distinction clear between titles and subtitles of books:

Blackberry Winter: My Earlier Years by Margaret Mead.

Colons are used between the hours and minutes when denoting time:

I'll pick you up at 7:45.

Last, but not least, the colon is used between the elements in proportions:

The ratio of sugar to flour is 1:4.

Exercise 1

All warmed up on commas, colons, and semicolons? In the following sentences, add all necessary punctuation. Remove unnecessary punctuation.

1. In the spring they plant crops in the fall they harvest them.

2. Luke loves his wife and other women love Luke.

3. Even if you disagree wait until the other person has finished speaking.

4. Her grandmother, who lives in India, has written a book her other grandmother is also a writer.

5. We have three cats Scout Bear and Truck.

6. I am looking for a good, used car.

7. If it starts to rain I will not drive to Boston my sister however will.

8. The teacher expected a lot, from her students, and for the most part she was not disappointed.

The Dash

A dash is used to set off a parenthetical phrase for emphasis or dramatic effect. Like the exclamation point, it is used far more often in creative writing and personal communications than in formal or professional situations.

"I know nothing—nothing in the world—of the hearts of men. I only know that I am alone—terribly alone." (Ford Madox Ford, *The Good Soldier*)

Let's change the punctuation and see what happens.

"I know nothing (nothing in the world) of the hearts of men. I only know that I am alone; terribly alone."

The original is more forceful; the parentheses in the altered version subtly minimize the starkness of the phrase *nothing in the world*. Plus, in the original, the dash physically isolates the words *terribly alone* at the end of the line, which further emphasizes their meaning. This is an example of how punctuation can be used to create style as well as literal meaning. Watch for such variations in your reading.

Compare the following two sentences:

He was with her everywhere.

"He was with her—everywhere." Toni Morrison, *Beloved*

By forcing the reader to make a significant pause in the original sentence, Morrison adds both drama and a touch of mystery or suspense; the reader must wait a beat before the revelation of that final word. This emphasis adds power to the word after the pause. Take away the hesitation and you get a more ordinary sense of the word *everywhere*.

The Parentheses

Use parentheses (and you're not going to use them very often) when you want to make brief comments, asides, or explanations that aren't crucial to the meaning of your sentence. The material in parentheses is less closely connected to your main idea than material you might set off with commas or dashes. This is largely a question of style. Parentheses are especially good when you want to:

1. minimize the contents of the message; or
2. insert a humorous or sarcastic comment

Parentheses are also more obvious (duh!) and intrusive than commas. Use them sparingly.

The Hyphen

1. **Use a hypen to indicate a word break between syllables at the end of a line.** If you cannot fit in the entire word that ends a line of print in your text (or in your handwritten communications, if you know what that quaint term refers to), insert a hypen between syllables and continue the word on the next line. Many computers can take care of such breaks automatically; refer to a dictionary if you need help deciding for yourself where to break up a word. A one-syllable word is never divided.

    > The concert started late, the band was surly, and before long pan-
    > demonium broke out.

2. **Use a hyphen to join two or more words acting as a unit when they appear before a noun:**

    > I can't stand *off-key* singing.

    > He missed their *late-night* suppers and long talks.

The *light-colored* dress suited her perfectly.

BUT: Many of her dresses were light colored.

The reason you hyphenate before the noun is to avoid any possible confusion. If you didn't hypenate *light-colored* and just put a comma or no punctuation between the two adjectives, you might think that the dress was light in weight and that it was colored. The hypen ensures your understanding that the dress was of a pale hue.

When the same adjectives appear after the noun, you no longer have this ambiguity, and therefore don't need a hyphen to make your meaning clear. In fact, if you wanted to suggest a dress that was light in weight, you would have to insert *and* between the two adjectives.

One more example. When some language experts compile lists of "bloopers" that they swear have actually appeared in print somewhere, headlines such as the following often appear:

Squad Helps Dog Bite Victim

This sounds like the squad assisted the dog in its attack. (We swear it wasn't Fido, our beloved Grammar Dog, going after someone who used a dangling modifier.)

What the editors meant (we assume) was that the squad gave assistance to the victim of a dog bite. Dog Bite is being used as an adjective before the noun Victim. Therefore, it needs a hyphen to show the two words are acting as a unit. Had this headline (if it ever was a real headline to begin with) been punctuated more precisely, it would have read:

Squad Helps Dog-Bite Victim

The meaning, in this case, is clear and unambiguous. In conversation, this sentence would not present a problem. Try saying both versions aloud and listen to the differences. In spoken English, your pauses and emphases naturally change to indicate your meaning. (Without a hyphen, you pause between *dog* and *bite*, and you stress the word *victim*. With a hyphen, you don't stop between *dog* and *bite*, and you stress *dog-bite* more than *victim*.)

Amazing, isn't it, what a little punctuation can do?

Exercise 2

In the following sentences, pace yourself for punctuation—especially hyphens, parentheses, and dashes. Add what is missing and remove incorrect punctuation. Some sentences may be correct. Some sentences may have more than one correct solution.

1. The well-known author arrived drunk.

2. Heather—works hard at the museum; so does Craig, her assistant.

3. I'm impressed with the hospital's up to date procedures.

4. He is well-known around here.

5. Rudy's biggest booster was himself surprise, surprise.

6. The committee keeps an up to date file on all contributors.

7. Unfortunately, her qualifications M.D., Ph.D. did not make up for her personality.

8. The star crossed lovers were separated once again.

9. Butterfly believed Pinkerton—completely.

The Apostrophe

Apostrophes are used in the following ways:

1. **In contractions.** An apostrophe indicates one or more missing letters in a contraction, a word formed by combining two other words.

    I + am = I'm (the *a* has been omitted)

    you + are = you're (the *a* has been omitted)

    he + will = he'll (the *wi* has been omitted)

    did + not = didn't (the *o* has been omitted)

will + *not* = *won't* (Fooled you! Usually the spelling doesn't change, but there are exceptions.)

Note that the following examples require an acute ear:

> *would've* = *would* + *have*
> (not *would of*)
>
> *could've* = *could* + *have*
> (not *could of*)
>
> *should've* = *should* + *have*
> (not *should of*)

It's or Its?

Anytime you use the word *it's* as a contraction, test it out by substituting the two words it stands for: *it is*. If the sentence doesn't make sense, you need to write *its*, the possessive.

---

2. **In possessives.** A possessive is used to show ownership or belonging. You can show this relationship by using certain words: the laughter of my niece; the building that belongs to Jeff; or the new motorcycle owned by my father.

Another common way to show possession is to add an apostrophe + *s* to the end of the word that names the owner: my *niece's* laughter; *Jeff's* building; or my *father's* new motorcycle.

This rule works for all *singular* owners, even if their names end in *-s*, *-z*, *-ch*, etcetera. For example:

> the church's interior
>
> Charles's four children
>
> Mumtaz's acting career

Most plural nouns end in *-s*. To make them into possessives, just add an apostrophe:

> the girls' car (more than one girl owns it)
>
> ten dollars' worth of gas
>
> the Thomases' children

For irregular plural nouns (those NOT ending in -s), you need to add an apostrophe + -s.

the *children's* toys

women's rights

Remember that pronouns have a separate form to show possession. The following list makes up what we call possessive pronouns: *my, your, his, her, its, our, their, mine, yours, his, hers, its, ours,* and *theirs.*

Be careful when expressing ownership of one *thing* by another *thing.* If you aren't careful, your sentence can easily be awkward and unclear.

The car's wheel was unusual. (awkward)

The wheel of the car was unusual. (better)

Their building's yard was a mess. (awkward)

The yard of their building was a mess. (better)

The spices' odor lured me into the shop. (awkward)

The odor of the spices lured me into the shop. (better)

Exercise 3

In the following sentences, do whatever is necessary to make each possessive or contraction correct. Make contractions wherever possible. Remove unnecessary or misplaced apostrophes.

1. Lewis' argument convinced the manager to increase security.

2. Its raining again; the porch's floor will get drenched.

3. Her parents wishes' had governed her every move.

4. Wont you join us at our familys' summer home this year?

5. I couldv'e told you that Buzz' teacher would win that award.

6. Is this not funny?

7. The evergreen shed it's needles all over the yard.

8. "A boys best friend is his mother."

Quotation Marks

Indeed. Life would be much duller if we couldn't occasionally listen in on what people (real people or fictional characters) were saying to one another. Whether in a newspaper article or a term paper, a novel or a business report, direct quotations enliven the story.

1. **Use quotation marks to set off the exact words of a speaker or writer.**
   Follow these patterns:

   Jane said, "_____."

   "_____," Jane said.

   "_____," Jane said, "_____."

In the first two examples, Jane speaks one sentence. In the third example, she still speaks only one sentence, but it is broken up in the middle by the identification of the speaker, or the *attribution*.

Now, in the following example, Jane says two sentences. Remember, a period signifies the end of a sentence. There are two periods here; therefore, you must have two sentences.

   "_____," Jane said. "_____."

Periods and commas always go inside the closing quotation marks. Colons and semicolons always go outside. The placement of question marks and exclamation points depends upon the content of the quotation.

> Marshall asked, "Do you like him?"

> Did she say, "I like him"?

When final punctuation must go outside the quotation marks to make your meaning clear, DO NOT also use final punctuation within the quotations. In other words, DO NOT write: Did she say, "I like him."?

> She screamed, "Stop!"

> I can't believe she said, "I want to move"!

> Patrick said, "I'm going to the mall"; Chloe refused to go with him.

To put quotations within quotations. When someone you are quoting quotes someone else, enclose the second quote in single quotation marks:

> Joseph asked, "Was it Shakespeare who wrote 'All the world's a stage'?"

> Mrs. Morse explained the situation: "Your father called and said, 'Could you please keep Adam an hour after school? I'm running late.' I assured him I'd be happy to stay with you until he arrived."

For indirect quotations. An indirect quotation is a restatement of the thoughts or comments of a person; it does not reproduce their exact words. Therefore, no quotation marks are used. An indirect quotation is often introduced by the word that. Compare the following:

DIRECT	**INDIRECT**
She said, "I'm going to be late."	She said that she was going to be late.
I thought, "If only I could spend three days alone on the beach.	I thought that it would be great if only I could spend three days alone on the beach."
He asked, "Could I be seated the near the window?"	He asked to be seated near window.

2. **Use quotation marks to indicate the titles of short works:**
   * **short stories:** "Araby" by James Joyce
   * **articles:** "Getting Down and Dirty for Science" by Richard Wolkomir
   * **poems:** "Despair" by Denise Levertov
   * **songs:** "Forever Young" by Bob Dylan

Titles of magazines, books, movies, and television and radio shows are italicized. If you are writing by hand or typing on a typewriter, underline these titles to indicate that they would be italicized in print.

Capitalization

In chapter 2, we discussed many of the situations in which you needed to use capital letters. Those were all nouns. Here are some other instances in which capital letters are called for.

1. **Capitalize the first letter of a new sentence. Or a fragment**. We know: in chapter 1, we told you not to use fragments. But sometimes you will use them, as we just did, for stylistic reasons. When you do, start them with a capital letter.

2. **Capitalize the first letter of a direct quotation**. For example:

   Casey cried, "Even if I am sick, you promised to take me to the circus!"

However, if you interrupt a sentence with an attribution, the second part of the quotation does not begin with a capital:

> "Even if I am sick," Casey cried, "you promised to take me to the circus!"

3. **Capitalize titles.** This is an arbitrary rule: Capitalize the first letter of all words *except* for short prepositions (fewer than five letters), short joining words (*and*, *but*, *or*, etcetera), and articles (*a*, *an*, *the*). However, the first letter of the first and last words in a title are *always* capitalized, regardless of the kinds of word they are.

Because nothing is gained in terms of clarity by this rule, some of us think it would make more sense to capitalize the first letter of every word in a title, but this is not the standard at present.

4. **Miscellaneous caps.** There are lots of other times you need to use capital letters, but we've covered the ones you'll encounter most often. If you are writing academic papers or need to know the rules for special situations, you can use one of the more exhaustive references we've listed in the back of this book under Power Sources. That's why these reference books exist: Even professional writers have to look up the rules sometimes. (Read: frequently.)

Exercise 4

Make all necessary corrections in the following sentences.

1. Have you read james dickey's poem the leap? asked Ron.

2. of course I have replied lucy it's one of my favorite poems.

3. The statement ask not what your country can do for you; ask what you can do for your country was first spoken by John F Kennedy at his Inauguration.

4. When I finish my work I sighed I'll be happy to go with you

Exercise 5

Correctly punctuate the following sentences.

"Could you stop by the campus tonight?" Professor Sherman asked his daughter Ginny. "I'll be glad to," she answered, "if you'll let me bring you dinner." Her father paused for a moment. He was distracted by several things happening all at once: a student knocking on his office door, a colleague waving an announcement in his direction, and a car alarm going off outside his window. "Are you still there, Dad? Dad?" Ginny shouted into the receiver. "Oh, sorry, dear," he muttered, "it's so busy here." He glanced around his office, which was a mess, and then he cheered up. "Let's just meet at a nice restaurant instead," he suggested.

Some Pleasures (and Perils) of English: Idioms and Troublesome Word Pairs

Idioms are the oddities of a language:

- You're putting me on.
- He kicked the bucket.
- Don't spill the beans.
- Keep your eyes peeled.

An idiom is a phrase or expression in a given language that is peculiar to itself. You can understand the meaning of each individual word and the grammatical construction of the entire phrase but not understand the idiom, because its meaning is greater than the sum of its parts. There's no car in the expression *"You drive a hard bargain."*

Plug In

Test your innate sense of language in the following exercise. Circle the correct choice in each sentence:

1. I argued (against, with) my brother about the death penalty.

2. Please (except, accept) this doctor's excuse for Troy's absence.

3. In many parts of the world, crowds would gather when murderers were (hung, hanged).

4. Arthur apologized and took (back, away) all the mean things he had said about me.

5. We arrived (to, at) the party just before midnight.

The Ego and the Id(iom)

When you study a second language, idioms can batter your ego because there are no clearcut principles with which to learn them. Each new encounter takes you by surprise. (Of course, that's also what makes idioms so much fun.) In your first language, you pick them up naturally by hearing others use them and by reading. Not only do you absorb their meaning, you gradually get a feel for the circumstances in which they are appropriate.

Usage and custom determine the form and meaning of idioms, which, once established, become accepted as integral parts of the standard language.

More on the Way It Is

There are many more idioms we can't explain either. But they have become ingrained in the landscape of our language. Read on, and have fun reading!

We like it when someone *turns us on* but not when they *turn on us*. However, we're generally neutral when they *turn on* a light. We want to *show up* at our friends' parties, but we don't want to *show them up*. *Up* and *down* are opposites, but *slow up* and *slow down* mean the same thing. A house *burns down*, but a piece of paper *burns up*.

Why do we *look up* the word in the dictionary instead of (the seemingly more logical) *look down*?

When we *wind up* a watch we are starting it, but when we *wind up* a conversation we're ending it. Yet, at the end of a long day, when we finally *wind up* at home, what's the first thing we want to do? *Wind down* or *unwind*.

In and *out* are also opposites, but that pickiest of institutions—the Internal Revenue Service—accepts our tax forms whether they have been *filled in* or *filled out.*

See and *look* are similar in meaning, but *oversee* and *overlook* are very different (although not quite opposites).

Watches, stockings, and noses don't seem to have anything in common, yet they all *run.*

And we can be *beside ourselves, under the weather,* or *on top of the world*—all without moving an inch.

So what gives? Go figure.

Getting a Feel for It

You can't learn idioms by mastering a set of rules. Idioms develop from the living, breathing, changing language, not from a memorized formula, and though you can try to memorize lists, you really learn idioms by listening and reading and practicing, because you have to get a *feel* for them.

But, you may ask, if we can't give you rules for idioms, why have a section about them? There are three reasons:

- We can list some of the trickier idioms so that you can be sure to use them correctly in your own work.

- We can expose you to the potential problems of idioms so you can become more aware of them. (Think of this as a consciousness-raising session.)

- Language is fun. We thought you'd enjoy seeing how vast and inexplicable some parts of it are.

Exercise 1

You've been sufficiently warmed up now on the power of idioms, so you're ready for your first exercise. What's wrong with each of the following sentences?

1. Harry is devoted for the piano, but he also has a strong interest with painting.

2. The coach was shocked to discover he was not immune from pressure.

3. Rachel has an abiding love and a scholarly interest in seventeenth-century poetry.

Use the Right Preposition

Often, the meaning of a verb or modifier stays the same, but when used with a different preposition, its meaning changes: sometimes slightly, sometimes significantly. In this section we'll examine how prepositions change the meaning of the following words (mostly verbs): *agree, angry, argue, compare, contrast, differ, different,* and *reconcile.*

1. **Agree:** We agree *to* a proposal; *on* a procedure; or *with* a person or a person's opinions/positions.

    > I'll *agree to* that proposal if we can *agree on* the procedures for implementing it.
    >
    > Zelda *agrees with* her yoga teacher; she *agrees with* everything the teacher says.

2. **Angry:** We become angry *at* or *about* a thing; and *with* a person.

    > Mason was *angry about* the foreclosure.
    >
    > Beverly was *angry at* their thoughtlessness.
    >
    > Conor was *angry with* me for leaving.

3. **Argue:** I argue *with* a person; and *for, against,* or *about* a measure, a point, a proposition, etcetera.

    > Stacey argued *against* the new tax laws; Seth argued *with* her but could not persuade her to change her mind.
    >
    > "Whether I *agree with* you, *argue with* you, or *get angry with* you, I still love you," Mom said.

4. **Compare:** We use *compare to* when looking only for similarities. Yet we use *compare with* when looking for similarities and differences.

> She liked to compare herself *to* great actresses of the past.
>
> Our high school baseball team compares favorably *to* other local teams.
>
> Al's cooking can't compare *with* his brother's.

5. **Contrast:** *Contrast with* creates a verb construction, whereas *in contrast to* creates a noun construction.

> Her pessimism *contrasts with* his optimism, but they seem to get along fine.
>
> His behavior toward his second wife is *in* stark *contrast to* his earlier antics.

6. **Differ:** One may *differ with* a person in an opinion, but *differ from* a person in appearance.

> I *differed with* him in my analysis of the economy.
>
> Jon *differs from* his father in looks: the former is tall and pale; the latter is short and dark.

7. **Different:** *Different from* is used before nouns or clauses. *Different than* is used before a clause (and used much less frequently than *different from*).

> Ralph is *different from* Roy.
>
> Ralph is *different from* the boy he used to be.
>
> Ralph is *different than* I remembered him.

8. **Reconcile:** We *reconcile to* a thing or event, but *reconcile with* a person.

> He became *reconciled to* his illness.
>
> She refused to *reconcile* herself *to* fate.
>
> Marcus was unexpectedly *reconciled with* his ex-wife.

To use the same preposition. If the same preposition applies to both nouns or verbs in a sentence, you don't need to repeat it. For example:

> He applied and was interviewed for the job.

Remember the paragraph about phrasal verbs in chapter 3? Phrasal verbs are so called because the verb stem itself consists of two or more words. Two-word stems *pair up* to create a new meaning: in other words, to create an idiom. Let's take another look at that paragraph.

> The kids *turned out* the light, *switched off* the radio, *clicked on* the TV, and *picked out* a video. "Well," said Mom, "at least they're not *running up* the phone bill." Dad laughed. "You're *putting* me *on*, right?" "I wouldn't *rule out* that possibility," smiled Mom.

There are only five sentences here, but it is power packed with idioms. Each of these matings of a verb and a preposition conveys a particular meaning. Sometimes the meaning is close to the meaning of the verb itself (*switched off*); sometimes it's quite different (*putting* me *on*).

One Phrasal Verb, Many Uses

Phrasal verbs are widely used in English. How widely? To give you an idea, let's look at just one verb—*to bring*. In the following sentence, *bring* is used in its literal sense ("to take or carry with oneself to a place") and *up* is used as an adverb of place.

> *Bring up* the laundry from the basement.

If you understand the literal meaning of each of these words, you can understand the meaning of the sentence.

> Transport the laundry from the room located on a lower level to a room on a higher level.

But look at these sentences:

> Iris didn't want to *bring up* the subject of money on their first date.

> Stuart had to *bring up* the children on his own.

Is the subject of money lurking in the basement? Are the children also lurking in the basement, along with the subject of money? No, of course not. In the case of Iris, *bring up* means introduce; in the case of Stuart, it means raise or rear.

How come you don't say *bring on* the subject or *bring out* the subject? *You just don't.* How do you know that? *You just do.* Unless, of course, English is not your first language, in which case you simply have to learn these idioms, just as native English speakers have to learn the idioms of other languages they're studying.

If English is your first language, you use most idioms without even thinking about them. If you are learning English as a second language, these are the little things that will *drive you crazy* (yet another idiom).

The following are examples of the phrasal verbs that can be made with the verb *bring*. Remember, a phrasal verb is a verb that consists of two words: In all these examples, the stem is *bring* plus another word.

1. **bring around or bring round** Used interchangeably, this phrasal verb can mean one of two things: to cause to adopt an opinion or take a certain course of action; or to cause to recover consciousness.

   > She finally *brought* her husband *around* to the idea of having a child.

   > After her fainting spell, the smelling salts *brought* her *round* immediately.

2. **bring down** The word *down* used with the verb *bring* means one of the following: to cause to fall from power or to collapse; to kill; or to lower something.

   > He was *brought down* by the assassin's bullet.

   > The political party was *brought down* by a military coup.

   > The stage manager decides when it's time to *bring down* the house lights.

3. **bring forth** To *bring forth* means to give rise to or produce. It also means to give birth to.

   Jerry *brings forth* incredibly lush vegetables from his backyard garden.

   At 6:00 p.m. the baby was *brought forth* into this world.

4. **bring forward** Any form of *to bring* with *forward* means one of two things: to present or produce; or, in accounting terms, to carry a sum from one page or column to another.

   Bring forward Her Majesty's jewels.

   Adam *brought forward* his totals from the previous page before he deciphered the balance.

5. **bring in** When combining the word *in* with the verb *to bring*, an idiom is created that means to submit a verdict in a court of law, or to produce, yield, or earn.

   The jury *brought in* a unanimous verdict of guilty on all counts.

   At his peak, he was *bringing in* over $200,000 a year.

6. **bring off** Simpler than the above examples, *bring off* has only one meaning: to accomplish.

   She was able to *bring off* raising her children while having a successful career.

7. **bring on** Here's another simple one, with one meaning only. To *bring on* means to cause to appear.

   The hostess clinked her glass and said, "*Bring on* the hors d'oeuvres! Let the party begin!"

8. **bring out** We're back to multiple meanings again. The phrasal verb *bring out* can mean: to reveal or expose; to produce or publish; or to nurture and develop (a quality, for example) to the best advantage.

> Last year she *brought out* her paintings, which had been in the attic for years.
>
> Her sixth novel was *brought out* a year ago.
>
> Caitlin's art teacher has *brought out* Caitlin's interest in painting trees.

9. **bring to** *Bring to* can mean: to cause to recover consciousness; or, in nautical terms, to cause (a ship) to turn into the wind or come to a stop.

> He was able to *bring* her *to* with mouth-to-mouth resuscitation.
>
> The sailboat was *brought to* in the small bay.

10. **bring up** The phrasal verb *bring up* can mean one of three things: to take care of or rear (a child); to mention or introduce into discussion; or, to vomit.

> She is busy *bringing up* her three children as a single parent.
>
> Did you have to *bring up* his drinking in the middle of dinner?
>
> Speaking of dinner, the 6-year-old *brought* hers *up* after running around too much.

We hope you're not sick of what the verb *bring* can do, because there's more! The following examples are all nonphrasal idioms. The single verb stem in these cases is *bring*, but it is modified by another word or phrase.

We *bring down the house* when we win overwhelming approval from an audience. Estelle's performance *brought down the house*. *Bring home* means to make perfectly clear. Michael Herr's book *brought home* the lasting impact of Vietnam on the men and women who served there.

When we use the phrase *bring to bear* we mean to exert or to apply. He *brought* financial pressure *to bear* on her decision. *Bring to light*, on the other hand, means to reveal or disclose. The reporter succeeded in *bringing to light* the candidate's meeting with a former mobster. *Bring to mind* means to cause to be remembered. "Your question *brings to mind* my own college days," said the lecturer.

What about *bring to (one's) knees*? This means to reduce to a position of subservience or submission.

> She vowed that no one would ever *bring* her *to her knees*.

If you *bring up the rear*, you'll be the last in a line or sequence.

> No matter how hard Dexter tried to keep up with the others, he was always *bringing up the rear*.

To *bring to terms* means to force (another) to agree. The secretary of state's mandate was to *bring* the two warring factions *to terms*. *Bring up short* means to cause to come to a sudden stop, literally or metaphorically. Murphy was *brought up short* by the accusation.

It's time to *bring up short* this discussion of *bring*!

And that was just one verb. Makes you realize how difficult English must be for nonnative speakers to learn.

Exercise 2

In the previous pages, we have put you through the paces. It's time for a long-distance run through the power of idioms. For each of the following verbs, write three idiomatic variations; state the meaning of each one; and write a sentence for each.

Example: to call

1. call off (cease)

> They called off the search at sunset.

2. call on (visit)

   We called on the new family to make them feel welcome.

3. call it quits (give up/separate)

   After fourteen years of marriage, Fred and Linda called it quits.

to give

   1. _____ (   )

   _____

   _____

   _____

   2. _____ (   )

   _____

   _____

   _____

   3. _____ (   )

   _____

   _____

   _____

to look

    1. _____ (   )

_____

_____

_____

    2. _____ (   )

_____

_____

_____

    3. _____ (   )

_____

_____

_____

to put

    1. _____ (   )

_____

_____

_____

    2. _____ (   )

_____

____

____

3. ____________________ (   )

____

____

____

TROUBLESOME WORD PAIRS

What follows is a somewhat arbitrary list of what we call verbal "imp-pairments"—or *imps*, for short, an *imp* being "a small demon" or "a mischievous child." These particular *imps* always come in *pairs*; that's how they trick you and *impair* your writing. (It's a little corny—okay, it's *really* corny —but if it helps you remember what to watch out for, who cares?)

These pairs can fool you because:

- They look alike.
- They sound alike.
- They're just plain confusing.

As a result, they can cause problems in diction, which means the correct word choice. You don't have to memorize this list, but glance through, circling the imps that have bedeviled you in the past. Add imps of your own. When you're not sure if you are using a word correctly, check the list for reassurance. If your imp does not appear on this list, look it up in the dictionary or try one of the additional resources we list in the back.

POWER SURGE

When you're not sure which preposition goes with a certain verb, look up the verb in the dictionary; the standard phrasal forms will be included.

The Imp List

1. **Accept/Except** *Accept* means to receive with consent or agree to something; *except* usually means other than (although it can also be used as a verb meaning to exclude).

    The store *accepted* all charge cards except American Express®.

    I'm disappointed in everyone, present company *excepted*.

2. **Adapt/Adopt** *Adapt* means to adjust to or to accommodate; *adopt* means to legally take a nonbiological child into one's family as one's own, or to accept or assume certain behaviors, standards, etcetera.

    Once we *adopted* the two boys, we naturally *adapted* to having children in the house.

    She *adopted* a theatrical style of speaking for a few years, then reverted to her more natural self.

3. **Advice/Advise** *Advice* is a noun, and it refers to the counsel or suggestions you give someone. *Advise* is the verb: to offer counsel or to make suggestions.

    He always asks me to *advise* him, but he rarely takes my *advice*.

4. **Affect/Effect** *Affect* is a verb meaning to influence or alter something; it can also mean to feign or pretend. *Effect* is a noun meaning the result; it can also be a verb meaning to bring to pass or to cause something.

    We were deeply *affected* by the girl's performance, which had a lasting *effect* on the children.

    He *affected* indifference, but he was deeply hurt.

    She worked to *effect* a lasting change in the health care industry.

5. **Aid/Aide** To *aid* means to give help or relief, or it means assistance; an *aide* is an assistant or helper.

   The *aide* stood by to *aid* the victims.

6. **Among/Between** *Among* is used for more than two people or things; *between* is used when referring to only two people or things.

   We had a lively discussion *among* the three of us, but then an argument broke out *between* Martin and me.

   He had to choose *between* the two horses.

   The scholarship winner will be selected from *among* the five finalists.

7. **Anxious/Eager** *Anxious* means worried or distressed. *Eager* means feeling or showing a keen desire.

   "We're so *eager* to see you," they wrote, "but *anxious* about your driving all that way by yourself."

8. **Borrow/Lend** You *borrow* from and *lend* to.

   May I *borrow* ten dollars until Monday?

   I'll be glad to *lend* you a novel to read on your trip.

9. **Breath/Breathe** *Breath* is the noun, the air you inhale and exhale. *To breathe* is the verb, to inhale and exhale air.

   All I wanted was a *breath* of fresh air, but my nose was so stopped up I could hardly *breathe*.

10. **Bring/Take** You *bring* to and *take* from.

   Bring a basket when you come to my house; I have lots of food for you to *take* home.

11. **Can/May** *Can* means you are able to do something; *may* indicates possibility or permission.

    Can you finish the assignment by Friday?

    You *may* use any of my books.

12. **Choose/Chose** *Choose* is the present tense; *chose* is the past tense.

    You *choose* which movie we see tonight; I *chose* last night.

13. **Compliment/Complement** *Compliment* can be a noun meaning praise or averb meaning to praise. *Complement* can also be a noun or a verb, meaning that which completes or goes well with something, or to add to or toenhance.

    I *compliment* you on this wine; it *complements* the fish perfectly.

    Hint: A compliment is a nice thing you say. To com*ple*ment something is to com*ple*te the picture.

14. **Corps/Corpse** A *corps* (pronounced kôr) is a group of people acting under common leadership or direction (especially in the military). A *corpse* (pronounce everything but the **e**) is a dead body.

    The rescue *corps* found a *corpse* in the rubble of the building.

15. **Desert/Dessert** A *desert* is a barren, desolate, or sandy area of land; a *dessert* is a sweet course that is served at the end of a meal.

    While crossing the *desert*, they had only dried fruit for *dessert*.

    ─○◌ᴡᴡ○ **SPARK** ○ᴡᴡ◌○─

    A person who is rightly punished for something is said to get his "just *deserts*." It's spelled like the barren place but pronounced like the thing you eat.

16. **Disinterested/Uninterested** If you're *disinterested*, you are impartial, neutral, or dispassionate. If you're *uninterested*, you're bored, apathetic, or indifferent.

   He hoped the judge would remain *disinterested*; he feared the jury had become *uninterested* in the case.

17. **Elude/Allude** *Elude* means to avoid, to slip away from, or to escape detection. *Allude* has a similar pronunciation but means to refer to something indirectly.

   He *alluded* to our past relationship, saying I had tried to *elude* him.

18. **Emigrate/Immigrate** You *emigrate* from a place; you *immigrate* to a place.

   Rosa is an *emigrant* from Kiev; she is an *immigrant* in Los Angeles.

19. **Farther/Further** *Farther* refers to physical distance; *further* indicates a greater degree or extent.

   On a good day, Carl Lewis can jump *farther* than anyone else; if you disagree, we can discuss this *further* over dinner.

20. **Flaunt/Flout** *Flaunt* means to show off; *flout* means to disregard or defy.

   Although she loved to *flaunt* her new clothes, she would never consider *flouting* the law.

21. **Fortuitous/Fortunate** *Fortuitous* means accidentally or by chance; *fortunate* means lucky or having a positive outcome.

   They were *fortunate* to have become such a good friends, especially since their initial meeting had been entirely *fortuitous*.

22. **Hanged/Hung** *Hanged* is the past tense of the verb *to hang* only when it refers to the act of executing a person; if you want to *hang* curtains, pictures, rigging, etc. you say it was *hung*.

> Before the murderer was *hanged* for his crimes, he was allowed to kiss the chain that *hung* from his wife's neck.

Even in slang, the past tense of *hang* is *hung*.

> We all *hung* out at the Sugar Shack.

23. **Incredible/Incredulous** *Incredible* means astonishing, implausible, hard to believe; *incredulous* means skeptical or disbelieving.

> I love when *incredible* things happen to me, but I remain *incredulous* about things I hear of second hand.

24. **Irritate/Aggravate** *Irritate* means to annoy. *Aggravate* means to make worse.

> It *irritates* me when you keep scratching that scab because I know it will *aggravate* the infection.

25. **Imply/Infer** The speaker/writer *implies*; the listener/reader *infers*.

> I *inferred* from her speech that she was politically progressive; she *implied* that she might run for the Senate next year.

26. **Literally/Figuratively** *Literally* means actually; *figuratively* means metaphorically. People often confuse the two. They say *literally* because they think it emphasizes their point: The afternoon sun *literally* turned her hair to gold, or he *literally* jumped out of his skin. Both are impossible except in fairy tales, comics, movies, etcetera. What is meant in both cases is "figuratively" or "it seemed as if."

She was *literally* an hour late.

His departure had *figuratively* torn her to pieces. (Chances are you would leave out the word *figuratively* here, the reader would infer [see above] that you didn't mean this literally.)

27. **Loose/Lose** *Loose* is a modifier meaning unattached; to *lose* is a verb meaning to fail to win or to fail to retain possession of something.

    Be careful not to *lose* all that *loose* change in your pocket.

28. **Nauseated/Nauseous** *Nauseated* means feeling sick to your stomach; *nauseous* means sickening, or causing nausea.

    I'm *nauseated* by the *nauseous* smell of that gasoline.

29. **Passed/Past** *Passed* is the verb form meaning to walk or go by a certain point. The *past* is a noun; it names a period of time that is over.

    He *passed* by his old house without ever thinking about the *past*.

30. **Principal/Principle** *Principal* (used as a noun) refers to an important person or one in charge of a school. It can also describe an interest-bearing amount of money. As an adjective, *principal* means the quality of being first in importance or rank. A *principle* is a basic truth, standard, or belief.

    The *principal* of the school is a pal to the kids; the *principles* she upholds are rules for living a decent life.

    The *principal* cause of death among that age range is cigarette smoking.

31. **Spade/Spayed** A *spade* is a garden tool used for digging. The verb is *to spade*, meaning to dig with a spade. There is another verb, entirely different: *to spay*. It means to neuter a female animal by removing her ovaries. (Male animals are castrated, but don't say this around Fido; he gets upset.)

We need to *spay* Gremlin so she won't have kittens.

Arnie *spaded* the garden in the morning, and in the afternoon he took his cat to the vet to be *spayed*.

It's kind to have your animals *spayed*; it's cruel to have them *spaded*.

32. **Stationary/Stationery** If you *stay* in one place, you are station*a*ry with an *a*; if you write a letter, you use station*e*ry with an *e*.

I need to buy more *stationery* if I'm going to be *stationary* with this broken leg for such a long time.

33. **Than/Then** *Than* is used to indicate a comparison. *Then* means next in order or time.

Monica runs faster *than* Marilyn. First do your homework, *then* watch the videotape.

Back *then*, I was bigger *than* you.

Hint: When in doubt about *then* and *than*, look at the spelling. The time words both contain -*hen*. When did it happen? T*hen*.

34. **Weather/Whether** *Weather* is the state of atmospheric conditions, or a verb meaning to endure, to come through. *Whether* indicates an alternative possibility or possibilities.

No one knows *whether* the *weather* will be better tomorrow.

We can *weather* any storm, literal or figurative.

35. **Who's/Whose** Who's is a contraction: *who* + *is* – *i* = *who's*; or *who* + *has* – *ha* = *who's*. *Whose* is a possessive pronoun. Remember, unlike nouns, when pronouns become possessive they do NOT take an apostrophe. Anytime you write *who's* with an apostrophe, test yourself by saying *who is* or *who has*. If this doesn't fit in your sentence, write *whose*.

Who's [*Who is*] the new boy?

Who's [*Who has*] got the key?

Whose car is this?

Who's going to be the next patient *whose* operation is botched by this incompetent surgeon?

36. Use/Used to *Use* means to employ, consume, or avail yourself of something; *used to* indicates a former state or customary practice.

We *used to* speak carelessly; now we *use* language more precisely.

The Worst Sins

Copy this sentence and tape it over your desk as a reminder of how NOT to spell when creating credible prose:

It is not **alright** to drink **alot** of **lite** beer to get you **thru** a hard **nite**.

Exercise 3

You are now powered up, ready for this test on troublesome words! Circle the correct word in parentheses.

1. Increased stress can (irritate, aggravate) certain medical conditions; my doctor's refusal to believe me (irritates, aggravates) me.

2. She said I was much more stubborn (than, then) my sister, but (than, then) she added that stubbornness wasn't always a bad quality.

3. It is easy to (loose, lose) (loose, lose) change.

4. The school (principle, principal) (complimented, complemented) me on my science project.

UNCONVENTIONAL SPELLINGS

This doesn't really go here, but it doesn't really go anywhere else in this book either and we're determined to make this point.

Unless an advertising agency is paying you big bucks to invent clever, eye-catching (read: unbearably kute) spellings of words—don't. Follow the standard dictionary spelling.

Exercise 4

It's been fun and a workout, going through all those idioms and tricky word pairs. You are now ready for this grammar power end-of-chapter quiz! Circle the correct answer in parentheses in each of the following sentences. For extra credit, underline any idioms that appear outside the parentheses.

1. (Whose, Who's) coming with me to pick (out, up) the grocery order that we phoned (out, in) earlier?

2. I'll agree (with, to) your proposal if you make one change: The secretaries should be allowed to order (stationary, stationery) when they see fit.

3. Kelly was angry (at, with) Peggy for always being late; after several years, she finally reconciled herself (with, to) the fact that she couldn't control her friend's behavior.

4. As an actor, Lars was not immune (from, to) the barbs of the theater critics.

5. I (implied, inferred) from his speech that all four of his grandparents had (immigrated, emigrated) from the area outside Kiev.

6. Was Carol putting us on when she said she received (advice, advise) from the president?

CHAPTER EIGHT

Prose and Cons: Some Tips for Strong, Clear Writing

In this chapter, we'll suggest some things to do (and *not* do) to strengthen your writing. The topics we'll discuss are parallel structure, wordiness, pompous language, and clichés.

Plug In

In each of the following sentences, words or phrases have been underlined. If they are grammatically correct and suitable for the sentence, do nothing. If they are not correct or not suitable, change them. Watch out for inflated or redundant language!

> ∿∿ **POWER LINE** ∿∿
>
> "Make everything as simple as possible, but not simpler."
>
> —Albert Einstein

1. He was known for his debating skill, <u>he writes well</u>, and his acting ability.

2. <u>The consensus of opinion</u> was that Harold was <u>stubborn in nature.</u>

3. <u>At this point in time</u>, Heather is ready for any challenge.

4. The baseball player excused himself for <u>expectorating</u> on the little kid's shoe.

5. Have you been studying for the <u>SAT test</u>?

PARALLEL STRUCTURE

It is important to express similar ideas in similar form. In other words: If there's a pattern, follow it. One of the goals of a good writer is to keep the reader on track at every point in the sentence: Don't allow any wrong turns.

~∿∿∿ **POWER LINE** ∿∿∿~

"When I was a lark, I sang;
When I was a worm, I devoured."
                    —Theodore Roethke,
                    "What Can I Tell My Bones?"

"The excursion is the same when you go looking for your sorrow as when you go looking for your joy."
                    —Eudora Welty, *The Wide Net*

Can you see the pattern in the lines from this well-known poet?

When I was a (*noun*), I (*past tense of a verb*).

Plug your own words into this pattern. For example:

When I was a goat, I chewed.

Eudora Welty's pattern sets a reader up for two alternatives, with the words *same* and *as*. Notice the parallel structure of the two alternatives. The excursion is the *same* (1) when you go looking for your sorrow *as* (2) when you go looking for your joy.

This pattern is easy to see and power packed with meaning!

KEY WORDS FOR PARALLEL STRUCTURE

Sometimes, *pairs of key words alert you to the fact that a parallel is being set up:*

> either . . . or
>
> neither . . . nor
>
> not only . . . but also
>
> not only . . . also

These pairs always go together; don't use the first half and then forget the second. Also, each part of the pair belongs immediately before the word(s) it modifies.

You may go to either the concert or the play. (Concert and play are objects of the preposition *to*.)

He is neither reliable nor friendly. (Reliable and friendly are both adjectives.)

Sally speaks not only well but also passionately. (Both well and passionately are adverbs.)

Watch Yourself!

What's wrong with this sentence:

> I like to play tennis and watching baseball.

It sounds awkward, doesn't it? We're set up by the subject and verb (*I like*) to expect one or more objects. But when we actually discover these objects, they come in two different forms: one is the infinitive (*to play*) and the other is a gerund (*watching*). In a given sentence, we expect similar things to take similar forms. When they don't, it's kind of like dressing the members of your basketball team in different-colored jerseys: it's disconcerting, if not downright confusing.

Or, to use our earlier theatrical analogy: Breaking the parallelism is like dressing three members of the cast in contemporary costumes and one in a Roman toga. We're not saying you should *never* do it, but you better have a good reason or the audience is going to boo and hiss.

Parallel structure improves the clarity and flow of normal, everyday speech and writing. Here are two ways to solve the above problem:

> I like to *play* tennis and *watch* baseball.

> I like *playing* tennis and *watching* baseball.

In the first solution, the *to* appears only once, but it is implied for the second verb as well. You could repeat the *to*, but you'd create a more formal tone.

> ○√w̸v○ **POWER LINE** ○√w̸v○
>
> "If thine enemy be hungry, give him bread to eat; and if he be thirsty, give him water to drink."
>
> —Proverbs, 25:21–22

Introductory Words: Another Peril of Parallels!

When you list three or more things in parallel, pay attention to introductory words: the *to* of an infinitive; articles (*a, an, the*), and prepositions. You have two choices: Use the introductory word only once, at the beginning of the list, or else use the word (or that type of word) in front of every item in the list.

Correct: I spent time *in* Paris, Barcelona, and Istanbul.

Correct: I spent time *in* Paris, *in* Barcelona, and *in* Istanbul. (Repeating *in* emphasizes each separate excursion.)

Wrong: I spent time *in* Paris, Barcelona, and *in* Istanbul. (This throws off the parallelism of the sentence and the implied sequence the reader expects.)

Of course, if there's a reason to interrupt your parallel—for dramatic effect, surprise, emphasis—by all means do so. That's the beauty of writing: Once you understand the "rules," you begin to see when breaking them can be effective. We said this way back in the first chapter.

> ○√w̸v○ **SPARK** ○√w̸v○
>
> Perhaps you've seen a sign like this posted in a diner somewhere:
>
> **Dinner Special**
>
> *Baked chicken $5.95; Turkey $6.95; Roast Beef $7.95; Children $4.00.*
>
> (Tempting, but we'll pass . . . .)

Because parallel structure sets up a pattern in terms of both rhythm and content, it is often used in poetry, proverbs, jokes, sermons, and speeches, as well as everyday conversation.

Conversely, be careful NOT to set things up in parallel if they are not equivalents. You may mislead someone.

Exercise 1

Get the idea? Here's a parallel exercise! Revise the following sentences using parallel structure to express parallel ideas. If the sentence does not require any revision, put a check mark beside it.

1. Our personalities are shaped by both heredity and what type of environment we have.

    _____

    _____

2. Willis works full time, coaches Little League, is gardening every weekend, and writes articles for his local newspaper.

    _____

    _____

3. Harry is a man with the best intentions and who has the highest principles.

    _____

    _____

4. The secretary must attend all meetings, call the roll, and keep the minutes.

    _____

    _____

5. Neither the pleas of the editorial writers nor what the demonstrators threatened to do affected Judge Solomon's decision.

    _____

    _____

A FEW WORDS ABOUT WORDINESS

Although it may sound contradictory at first, Pascal's explanation makes sense when you think about it: It is far more difficult to write something that is brief and to the point than it is to write something long and rambling. Why? Because the former requires thought, planning, and revision. The latter requires only that you spill out everything that comes to mind.

○ᗧᗧᗧ **POWER LINE** ᗧᗧᗧ○

"This letter is so long because I lacked the time to make it short."

—Blaise Pascal

Here are some suggestions to help you combat flabby writing.

Writing Tip 1: In General, Use Single Words Instead of Phrases

Somewhere along the line, many of us picked up the idea that the following phrases sounded more "sophisticated" or "intelligent" than their shorter equivalents. We were wrong.

Instead of	Use
owing to the fact that	since
in spite of the fact that	although
in connection with	about
with respect to	about
as a result of	because
for the reason that	because
due to the fact that	since
in the month of May	in May
at the present time	now
at this point in time	now
be in a position to	be able to
in the event that	if

Instead of	Use
make a decision	decide
in order to	to
by means of	by
in view of the fact that	since
during the time that	while/when
for the purpose of	for
held a meeting	met
expert in the field of	expert in
means to imply	implies
because of the fact that	because
have need of	need
give encouragement to	encourage
for the purpose of	for
make an adjustment in/to	adjust
seems/appears to be	seems/appears
give consideration to	consider
consider to be	think/believe
is of the opinion	thinks/believes
along the lines of	like
in the amount of	for
make inquiry regarding	inquire/ask
on the occasion of	when
in the case/event that	if

Be wary of the *not un-* construction. We often use what are called *double negatives* to make a certain point.

> He was a *not* unfriendly man.
>
> He was *not* unattractive.
>
> She was *not* uncooperative.

These sentences are fine if you're trying to convey a sense of great reluctance about acknowledging these qualities in the subjects, or if you want to highlight the extreme slightness of the quality under discussion. But if you don't want to damn your subject with faint praise, speak positively and succinctly:

> He was a friendly man.
>
> He was attractive.
>
> She was cooperative.

To correctly use or drop *who/whom* or *that* after a noun. Use your judgment, but sometimes it's not necessary to use *who/whom* or *that* after a noun:

> The woman whom I bought the car from is my boyfriend's aunt.
>
> The woman I bought the car from is my boyfriend's aunt. (smoother)
>
> The first problem that we tackled was exceptionally difficult.
>
> The first problem we tackled was exceptionally difficult. (smoother)

Exercise 2

Keep your writing muscles taut and lean! Cross out all unnecessary words or rewrite to shorten the following sentences.

1. She seems to be of a reclusive nature.

_____

_____

2. He made inquiries in regard to the not inexpensive tour package.

_____

_____

3. Please give consideration to the speech that was delivered by Buddy.

_____

_____

4. He got there by means of an automobile. (For extra credit: Reduce this sentence to two words.)

_____

_____

Writing Tip 2: Avoid Redundancies

Redundancy is a particular form of wordiness. It means repeating the idea you want to convey (as opposed to just puffing it up with extra words).

Redundant	Concise
attractive in appearance	attractive
attractive appearance	attractive
	Attractive automatically refers to appearance or overall impression unless otherwise stated. If you want to focus on some other specific quality, then name it: Ronnie's outlook on life was attractive to me; Ronnie was attractive, too.
green in color	green
tall in height	tall
charming in character	charming

Redundant	**Concise**
suspicious in nature	suspicious
in an eager manner	eagerly
endorse on the back	endorse

Endorse means "to sign something on the back," so there's no need to add the *on the back* part. It also figuratively means "to support or give backing to" something or someone: "I endorsed her candidacy."

end result	result
final outcome	outcome
advance notice	notice
general consensus	consensus

Consensus means "a general opinion or agreement," so there's no need to repeat it!

advance warning	warning
young juvenile	juvenile
refer back	refer
return back	return
revert back	revert
reflect back	reflect
cooperate together	cooperate

Cooperate means "to work together."

descending down	descending
ascending up	ascending
consensus of opinion	consensus
modern world of today	the modern world/today's world
fundamental principles	principles
root cause	cause

Redundant	Concise
repeat over	repeat
repeat over again	repeat

Repeat is to do or say something for a second time, right? Therefore, to repeat over is to do it for a third time—and to repeat over again is to do it for a fourth time! Of course, you might use this construction informally for emphasis (or without realizing it, as we've all done), but generally don't repeat yourself over again just for the heck of it.

Special Kinds of Redundancies

1. **Double comparisons.** Double comparisons are faulty on two grounds: 1) they're redundant; and 2) one form will be incorrect (you remember from chapter 4 that comparatives take one of two different forms).

   Avoid the following unless you're writing dialogue for a three-year-old:

   more smarter; more nicer; more funnier; most handsomest; most tallest.

2. **Misused abbreviations and acronyms.** We misuse abbreviations and acronyms when we don't know what the initials stand for or when we don't stop to think what we're saying or writing.
   - *HIV virus*: HIV stands for Human Immunodeficiency *Virus*, so don't add another *virus*.
   - *NATO organization*: NATO stands for North Atlantic Treaty *Organization*, so don't add another *organization*.
   - *NAFTA agreement*: NAFTA stands for North American Free Trade *Agreement*, so don't add another *agreement*.
   - *SALT talks*: SALT stands for Strategic Arms Limitation *Talks*, so don't add another *talks*.
   - *SAT test*: SAT stands for Scholastic Assessment *Test*, so don't add another *test*.
   - *ATM machine*: ATM stands for Automated Teller *Machine*, so don't add another *machine*.

These misuses become so widespread they often begin to sound normal; sometimes they even sound better than the technically correct version. "I used to be in favor of the NAFTA agreement," sounds more natural than "I used to be in favor of the NAFTA." The solution is to eliminate the article before the acronym: "I used to be in favor of NAFTA."

To avoid redundancies—especially in professional situations—you're better off not using an abbreviation or acronym unless you know exactly what it stands for.

Writing Tip 3: Use the Active Rather Than the Passive Voice

This suggestion came up in chapter 3, when we talked about how the use of the passive voice affected the meaning of the sentence. Here we are concerned solely with economics. (*Economics*? In a *grammar* book? Well, yes.) Consider this analogy: If you could get your car to run an equal distance on less gas, wouldn't you go for it? Why not do the same for your sentences?

> ∿∿○ **POWER SURGE** ○∿∿
>
> We do not mean to suggest that all your sentences should be short, or that you should eliminate the whole range of tools available to make your writing interesting, varied, precise, humorous, or beautiful. But, if the words aren't adding anything, omit them.

The sink was fixed by Marlene. (six words)

Marlene fixed the sink. (four words)

You have saved two words without sacrificing meaning, clarity, or tone. That's one-third of your total sentence length—a major streamlining that your readers will appreciate. Also, it's almost always more interesting to read an active voice rather than a passive voice.

> ∿∿○ **POWER LINE** ○∿∿
>
> "I am a Bear of Very Little Brain, and long words Bother me."
>
> A. A. Milne, *Winnie-the-Pooh*

Writing Tip 4: Regarding Pomposity

There is nothing inherently wrong with a long word. If it suits both the precise meaning you need and the tone you want to convey, then by all means use it. Problems arise when people pull such words—often only vaguely understood—out of their memory banks and fling them around like thousand-dollar bills, driven more by the desire to impress others with one's wealth than to make oneself understood. Very few people intentionally present themselves as arrogant, pompous, and foolish, but too often that is the effect of what Pooh refers to as "long words" on an audience.

Remember when smoking was allowed on airplanes? Did you ever wonder why before takeoff the flight attendants instructed you "to extinguish all smoking materials"? Why didn't they just say, "Put out your cigarettes"? The attendants never asked if you would care to "consume any eating materials." (Although that was what their food generally tasted like.)

Words *are* wealth: they should be enjoyed, played with, even experimented with. Your vocabulary should keep expanding throughout your life.

Just because two words are synonyms doesn't mean they are equally suited to all occasions. Much stilted language comes from two sources: the *insecurity* that drives us to try to impress an audience, and, as George Orwell argues in his famous essay, "Politics and the English Language," the *insincerity* that drives us to try to mislead an audience.

 **SPARK**

The best way to increase your word power is NOT by studying a dictionary but by reading. You will subconsciously pick up the meaning of most unfamiliar words from their context; if a word really stumps you, then go to the dictionary.

We're not going to give you a list of specific words here, because in the right situation, any single word may be absolutely the right choice. But *categories* of pompous words to avoid include the following.

Watch out for *multisyllablic* words. Many multisyllabic words have perfectly good shorter equivalents that will make your meaning both clear and natural-sounding. For instance, intead of *commodious*, use *roomy* or *spacious*.

Watch out for *foreign words* and *phrases*. Try to avoid using foreign words and phrases that have perfectly good English equivalents. "I punched him in the *solar plexus*" sounds more inflated than "I punched him in the stomach." If you have a good reason, use the foreign term.

~~~**POWER LINE** ~~~

Even Yogi Berra used French on occasion (well, at least one occasion): He's given credit for the much-quoted line, "It's déjà vu all over again."

Watch out for jargon. Jargon is the technical terminology used within a trade, profession, or similar group. It is usually too esoteric (and not that useful) for outsiders, but it can have a place among people sharing an intense, demanding, or highly specialized workplace. It's sometimes referred to as "clinical" language, suggesting that it has been stripped of any emotional connotation. Jargon that has made it to the mainstream language includes terms such as *downsize, interface, codependent,* and *revenue shortfall.*

~~~**POWER SURGE** ~~~

The best advice is this: Write to be understood, not to impress.

Exercise 3

Lift the pompous language right out of the following examples! Circle the word or phrase in parentheses that you think is more suitable for an informal personal essay. None of the words in parentheses are *wrong,* but some are obviously unsuitable in this context.

Annie was seven years old when her (*father, male parent*) died. She missed him and felt lonely inside the (*domicile, house*) where they had lived (*in conjunction with, together with*) the rest of the family. Annie's (*dog, canine companion*) comforted her, but when she had to (*relocate in, move to*) California, she (*cried, wept*) all day.

Writing Tip 5: Avoid Clichés

A cliché is a phrase or a saying that has become worn out through overuse. Clichés start out fresh. They are created in literature ("Brevity is the soul of wit," Shakespeare, *Hamlet*); song lyrics ("You don't need a weatherman to know which way the wind blows," Bob Dylan); slang ("Gag me with a spoon"); advertisements ("Where's the beef?"); TV shows ("Just the facts, ma'am"—which has been transformed in the last few years to "Just the fax, ma'am"); and movies ("Make my day."). Many that we still use derived from phrases written in the sixth century B.C.—in the *Fables* of Aesop: "a wolf in sheep's clothing," "sour grapes," "slow and steady wins the race."

⌇⌇⌇ SPARK ⌇⌇⌇

Pretentious-Language Jokes, Not to Be Confused with Pretentious Language-Jokes (see how important a hyphen can be?)

- *Doctor to new patient:* I understand you're here because you developed a pain in the lumbar region.

  Patient to doctor: No, I've never even been to the woods.

- *Lawyer to witness:* Ms. Johnson, is your appearance here this morning pursuant to a deposition notice delivered to your attorney?

  Witness to lawyer: No. This is how I always dress for work.

The problem is, when great expressions come along, we tend to treat them like our favorite pair of shoes: We wear them over and over until their soles (and their souls) wear out.

When that happens, we need to let them go. Although we admit, it'll take a genius to come up with a substitute for "it's on the tip of my tongue." Certainly, each of us relies on a few old standbys, especially when speaking, but try not to clutter your writing work with clichés. They're not *wrong*; they're just dull.

No list of clichés could begin to be complete, but the following lists will give you an idea of the various forms clichés take. Be on guard. Notice that clichés may also be idioms.

Clichéd Things You Can Be

tired but happy
happy as a clam
young at heart
old as the hills
bored to tears
sadder but wiser
slippery as a goose
free as a bird
high as a kite
a diamond in the rough
a disaster waiting to happen
thick as thieves
all thumbs
all ears

Clichéd Things You (or an Object) Can Do

sleep like a log
nip it in the bud
fall through the cracks
come to a head
draw a blank
make a killing
play hardball
beat a dead horse
chomp at the bit
bite the bullet
tip your hat to
harbor an illusion
push the envelope
toe the line
run it up the flagpole and see if anyone salutes

Clichéd Things You Can't Do

see the forest for the trees
take it with you

Just Plain Clichéd Things

a giant step forward
leaps and bounds
the bottom line
brute force
acid test
a long row to hoe
a hue and cry
the powers that be
a word to the wise
a sea of faces
a cloud of suspicion
the tip of the iceberg
a blessing in disguise
a fresh start
the bitter end

Clichéd Colors and Qualities

black as night
green as grass
pale as a ghost
white as a sheet
red as a rose
soft as silk
hard as a diamond
sturdy as an oak
clear as a bell
quick as a bunny

cold as ice
good as gold

The Natural World Through a Cliché Lens

a crisp, autumn *anything* (morning, air, day, evening, breeze)
a blanket of snow
sheets of rain
a pillow of earth
a mound of leaves
a bolt from the blue
broad daylight
the calm before the storm
shelter from the storm
steaming jungle
teeming jungle
blazing sun
blistering heat
the frozen North
howling wind
raging wind
endless sea
uncharted seas

Food for Thought (Itself a Cliché)

cool as a cucumber
apple-cheeked
bone of contention
a hill of beans
you can't make an omelette without breaking eggs
his goose is cooked
two peas in a pod
sweet as sugar

sweet as honey

sweet as pie

sweeter than wine

Clichéd Sayings

Life is a bowl of cherries.

It takes one to know one.

A rolling stone gathers no moss.

You can often add life to a cliché by twisting it into a pun. For example, the writer Dorothy Parker took the expresson "to run the gamut of emotions from A to Z" and changed it ever so slightly to create a devastating insult in one of her theater reviews. Speaking of a featured actress in a Broadway play, Parker wrote, "She ran the gamut of emotions from A to B."

You can do this, too. "Going to this party is *a fate worse than death*," you complain one evening as you're getting dressed. This is just another cliché. But if you twist it into, "This party will be a fête worse than death," it becomes a fresh and funny play on words. Clichés make great raw material for comedians who like to pun.

POWER LINE

When the great pitcher Satchel Paige was asked how fast he was, he responded by saying, "I'm so fast I can turn off the light switch on the wall and jump into bed before the room gets dark." That sure beats "quick as a bunny."

Exercise 4

Your battery should be fully charged now in the following areas: faulty parallelism, wordiness, redundancies, pompous language, and clichés. Rewrite the following paragraph, correcting for such weaknesses.

At the end of the month of October, I was forced to make a decision about my job. In view of the fact that my boss was not unwilling to discuss my different options with me, I approached her in connection with my future plans. She is a woman with high ethical standards and who has respect for the people in the company. "The majority of the projects here are of a temporary nature," she said in a reluctant manner. "The powers that be have me trapped between a rock and a hard place: I don't want to lose you, but I don't want you to harbor the illusion that there will still be work for you in six months' time. In view of the fact that you have worked well with your colleagues, your supervisors, and with your support staff, I'm of the opinion that you will be better off making a fresh start elsewhere."

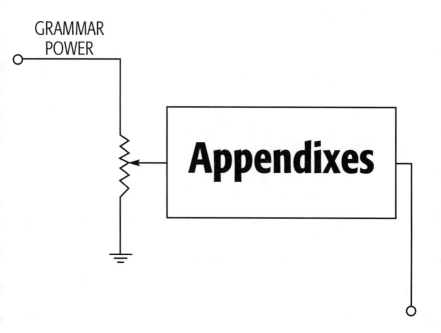

GRAMMAR
POWER

Appendixes

Answer Key

CHAPTER ONE

Plug In

1. <u>phone</u> is <u>ringing</u>
2. <u>you</u> <u>could answer</u>
3. <u>You</u> [implied] <u>do tell</u>; <u>I</u> <u>am</u>
4. <u>Mom and Dad</u> <u>will not ground</u>; <u>I</u> <u>will grind</u>
5. <u>Having a little sister</u> <u>tries</u>

Exercise 1

1. <u>We</u>
2. <u>roses</u>
3. <u>January and February</u>
4. <u>You</u>
5. <u>his voice</u>

Exercise 2

1. <u>screamed</u>
2. <u>has been trying</u>
3. <u>sings</u> / <u>plays</u>
4. <u>are going</u>
5. <u>lay</u>

Exercise 3

[<u>You</u>] <u>Make</u> my day. (**command**)

<u>Would</u> you <u>excuse</u> me? (**question**)

[<u>You</u>] Please <u>come</u> here. (**command**)

[<u>You</u>] <u>Stop</u> right there! (**command and exclamation**)

There <u>is</u> no <u>joy</u> in Mudville. (**statement**)

Exercise 4

1. <u>Margot and Tony</u> <u>demanded</u> a refund from the clerk <u>who</u> <u>had lost</u> their reservation.
2. <u>I</u> <u>traveled</u> through India.
3. When <u>I</u> <u>go</u> to my brother's house, his <u>dog</u> always <u>jumps</u> up and <u>licks</u> me on the face.
4. [<u>You</u>] <u>Sit down</u> and <u>make</u> yourself at home.
5. Does <u>Ruby</u> <u>yell</u> at everyone?
6. There <u>were</u> two <u>reasons</u> for Anna's resignation.
7. <u>David</u> <u>is</u> alone and <u>seems</u> sad today.
8. <u>Ellen and Chris</u> <u>are</u> my friends.
9. <u>She</u> <u>does</u> not <u>appear</u> sorry for what she did.
10. Where <u>is</u> <u>everyone</u>?

Exercise 5

Answers may vary.

1. trying to look out the window <u>subject and verb</u> (missing part)
   Rewrite: We were trying to look out the window.

2. a lot of cockroaches <u>verb</u>
   Rewrite: A lot of cockroaches invaded the apartment.

3. and seems like a nice person <u>subject and verb</u>
   Rewrite: Wyatt is friendly and seems like a nice person.

4. is nervous about the exam <u>subject</u>
   Rewrite: Lynn is nervous about the exam.

5. one by one <u>subject and verb</u>
   Rewrite: One by one, the students left the room.

6. in spite of all my efforts <u>subject and verb</u>
   Rewrite: In spite of all my efforts, the project was a day late.

7. after seeing the doctor <u>subject and verb</u>
   Rewrite: He felt better after seeing the doctor.

Exercise 6

Answers may vary.

1. (fragment) After we woke up, we ate breakfast.
2. (fragment) That cute boy wearing the green sweater is from Argentina.
3. (comma splice) I'm not going shopping; they never have what I want anyway.
4. (comma splice) She brought her boyfriend flowers; candy wasn't good for him.
5. (fused) He works hard on his papers because he wants to get all A's.
6. (comma splice)The dress doesn't fit, but I'll buy it anyway.
7. (fused) Sunshine is good for you; too much sun is bad for you.

CHAPTER TWO

Plug-In

1. To move to, <u>Seattle</u> would mean leaving a wonderful <u>group</u> of <u>friends</u>.
2. <u>Caitlin</u> threw <u>Nora</u> the <u>bouquet</u>.
3. <u>Pablito</u>, his only <u>grandchild</u>, ran to greet him.
4. Her <u>home</u> is <u>Brooklyn</u>; she has lived in the northern <u>tip</u> of that <u>borough</u> for <u>years</u>. [no capital *n* in *northern*]
5. Who was the <u>idiot</u> who let out the <u>monkeys</u>?

Exercise 1

1. Vinnie works at the Louvre.
2. Have you read *Crime and Punishment*?
3. Mike went to see *Star Wars*.
4. Everyone in Atlanta watches the Braves play.
5. "The Star-Spangled Banner" came on the radio.
6. Professor Humbert has stopped reading the *New York Times*.

Exercise 2

1. The movie was released on videotape.
2. The memorial draws thousands of visitors.
3. The student has been attending a university.
4. The man eats cereal every morning.
5. The woman loves to teach third grade.
6. The artist lives on through his paintings.

Exercise 3

1. subject
2. subject, object of preposition
3. indirect object of verb, direct object of verb, appositive
4. subject, indirect object of verb, direct object of verb
5. subject, complement
6. subject, appositive, direct object of verb
7. object of preposition, direct address

Exercise 4

My Only Child
Days of My Life
Little Woman
Of a Mouse and a Man
The Snow Goose
"Autumn Leaf"

Exercise 5

1. Kennedys
2. Martenses
3. Derbys
4. daughters-in-law
5. Christmases

Exercise 6

1. John, aunt, brother
2. Aunt Ida, aunt
3. school, transferring, University of Michigan
4. friend
5. Missouri
6. states, United States of America
7. doctor, doctor, Ph.D.
8. Paris, Eiffel Tower
9. Paris, spring
10. April, May

CHAPTER THREE

Plug In

plans
lie
is
is, asks
are, broken
making
were
tries
is

Exercise 1
1. weeps (intransitive)
2. seems (linking)
3. comforts (intransitive)

Exercise 2
1. are
2. were
3. has
4. are
5. pushes
6. is
7. lie
8. was
9. runs

Exercise 3
1. Change *shared* to *shares*
2. Change *sells* to *sold*
3. Change *rolled* to *roll*

Exercise 4
1. were
2. were
3. makes
4. is
5. was
6. are
7. like
8. attracts
9. Is
10. was
11. burst
12. organizes
13. wrote
14. was
15. had

CHAPTER FOUR

Plug In

1. me
2. We
3. I
4. whom
5. I
6. its
7. me

Exercise 1

1. I
2. her
3. (correct as is)
4. us
5. (correct as is)

Exercise 2

1. me
2. his
3. We
4. I
5. him and me
6. one's
7. their
8. them
9. her
10. whom

CHAPTER FIVE

Plug In

1. *quickly* modifies *learns*
2. *nervous* modifies *seem*
3. *really* modifies *tired*
4. *quietly* modifies *sit*
5. *well* modifies *did*
6. *likely* modifies *person*
7. *well* [not *good*] modifies *runs*
8. *beautiful* modifies *look*

Exercise 1

1. (adv) *beautifully* modifies the verb *dances*
2. (adj) *more* modifies the noun *soup*
3. (adv) *too* modifies the adjective *tired*
4. (adv) *usually* modifies the adjective *adventurous*
5. (adj) *another* modifies the noun *cup*
6. (adv) *fully* modifies the adjective *aware*
7. (adv) *initially* modifies the verb *put off by*
8. (adv) *later* modifies the verb *admired*
9. (adj) *frightened* modifies the noun *child*
10. (adj) *lingering* modifies the noun *doubts*

Exercise 2

1. (correct as is)
2. (correct as is)
3. lovingly
4. (correct as is)
5. angrily
6. angry (In this sentence, *angry* modifies the noun *Minnie*; therefore, it is an adjective.)

7. beautifully
8. (correct as is)
9. really

Exercise 3

the de*scrib*ed writer
the re*train*ed engineer
the de*light*ed electrician
the de*compos*ed songwriter
the dis*heart*ened organ donor
the de*bark*ed tree surgeon
the dis*concert*ed symphony conductor
the de*tour*ed travel guide
the de*test*ed teacher
the dis*tress*ed hair stylist

Exercise 4

Only he took the French course. (There is one student in the class.)

He **only** took the French course. (He registered; he sat there; but he didn't really study or apply himself in any meaningful way.)

He took **only** the French course. (He didn't take any other courses.)

He took the **only** French course. (Only one French course of any kind was offered.)

He took the French-**only** course. (The entire course was conducted in French.)

Exercise 5

Answers may vary.

1. Susanna said the book she had been reading bored her **quickly** to distraction.
2. Rushing to the theater, **I caught** my heel in the sidewalk and my heel broke.
3. **For you** to drive a tractor, your patience must match your skill.
4. I was very skeptical when she stated blithely that she reads **almost** an entire novel in one sitting.
5. To get into the good graces of management, **you must have** ability and loyalty **that are** evident and unquestionable.
6. When viewing it through a veil of smog, **you might find Los Angeles very impressive, according to the tourist brochure**.
7. Even the students who work hard do poorly **occasionally** in a testing situation.
8. While standing on station platforms, **you may see** high-speed trains pass in either direction at any time.
9. **While** driving through the back roads, we saw many deer.
10. **When I was** five, my grandmother told me about her escape from Chile to the United States.
11. Jeremy could not keep his eyes off the new painting **that was** hanging awkwardly on the wall above the sofa in his wife's office.

Exercise 6

1. *staggering* modifies the noun *opponent*; **adjective, correct**
2. *real* modifies the adjective *good*; **adverb; really**
3. *good* modifies the noun *apple pies*; **adjective, correct**
4. *well* modifies the verb *bakes*; **adverb, correct**
5. *Grazing on the hillside* modifies *herd of sheep*; **adjective phrase, I noticed a herd of sheep grazing on the hillside.**
6. *less* modifies the noun *students*; **adjective, fewer**

7. *At the age of six* modifies the speaker, the pronoun *I*; **adjective phrase**, When I was six, my father . . .

8. *While I was chatting on the phone* modifies the verb *overflowed*; **adverb, correct**

CHAPTER SIX

Plug In

Answers may vary.

1. Suzanne visited India, Pakistan, and Nepal; Kelly, however, visited only India.

2. "I'd be glad to manage your campaign," said Rhonda, "but I've never done anything that ambitious before."

3. Would anyone, including you children, like to help me out onstage?

4. Although it's an unusual request, the students' representative would like to address the faculty next Monday at 2:30.

5. The baby can have any of the following: milk, juice, bananas, or cookies.

Exercise 1

Answers may vary.

1. In the spring they plant crops; in the fall they harvest them.

2. Luke loves his wife, and other women love Luke.

3. Even if you disagree, wait until the other person has finished speaking.

4. Her grandmother who lives in India has written a book; her other grandmother is also a writer.

5. We have three cats: Scout, Bear, and Truck.

6. I am looking for a good used car.

7. If it starts to rain, I will not drive to Boston; my sister, however, will.

8. The teacher expected a lot from her students, and, for the most part, she was not disappointed.

9. "I'll get you, my pretty, and your little dog, too."

Exercise 2

Some answers may vary.

1. (correct as is)
2. Heather works hard at the museum; so does Craig, her assistant.
3. I'm impressed with the hospital's up-to-date procedures.
4. He is well known around here.
5. Rudy's biggest booster was himself (surprise, surprise).
6. The committee keeps an up-to-date file on all contributors.
7. Unfortunately, her qualifications—M.D., Ph.D.—did not make up for her personality.
8. The star-crossed lovers were separated once again.
9. (correct as is)

Exercise 3

1. Lewis's argument convinced the manager to increase security.
2. It's raining again; the floor of the porch will get drenched. (Porch's is not technically incorrect, but it sounds awkward.)
3. Her parents' wishes had governed her every move.
4. Won't you join us at our family's summer home this year?
5. I could've told you that Buzz's teacher would win that award.
6. Isn't this funny?
7. The evergreen shed its needles all over the yard.
8. "A boy's best friend is his mother."

Exercise 4

1. "Have you read James Dickey's poem 'The Leap'?" asked Ron.
2. "Of course I have," replied Lucy. "It's one of my favorite poems."
3. The statement, "Ask not what your country can do for you; ask what you can do for your country," was first spoken by John F. Kennedy at his inauguration.
4. "When I finish my work," I sighed, "I'll be happy to go with you."

Exercise 5

Answers may vary.

"Could you stop by the campus tonight?" Professor Sherman asked his daughter Ginny. "I'll be glad to," she answered, "if you'll let me bring you dinner." Her father paused for a moment. He was distracted by several things happening all at once: a student knocking on his office door, a colleague waving an announcement in his direction, and a car alarm going off outside his window. "Are you still there, Dad? Dad!" Ginny shouted into the receiver. "Oh, sorry, dear," he muttered. "It's so busy here." He glanced around his office, which was a mess, and then he cheered up. "Let's just meet at a nice restaurant instead," he suggested.

CHAPTER SEVEN

Plug In

1. with
2. accept
3. hanged
4. back
5. at

Exercise 1

1. Harry may long for the piano, look for the piano, pay for the piano, or arrange for the piano to be moved into his studio, but he is *devoted to* the piano. He can have an involvement with painting, a love affair with painting, or a struggle with painting, but he has an *interest in* painting.
2. The coach can escape from pressure or explode from pressure, but he is not *immune to* pressure.
3. The problem in this sentence stems from the compound object. Rachel has two things: a genuine love and a scholarly interest. Rachel quite rightly has an *interest* in poetry, but she can't have a *love in* poetry—that is not idiomatic. Therefore we have to add a separate preposition to follow *love*. Rachel can have a *love for* poetry, so you need to include this preposition in the sentence also. Rachel has a genuine *love for* and a scholarly *interest in* seventeenth-century poetry.

Exercise 2

Answers may vary.

to give

1. give in (capitulate, yield)
2. give up (quit, surrender)
3. give out (cease functioning)

to look

1. look into (investigate)
2. look out for (be careful of)
3. look up to (admire)

to put

1. put off (postpone)
2. put down (insult)
3. put away (store in a proper place)

Exercise 3

1. aggravate; irritates
2. than; then
3. lose; loose
4. principal; complimented

Exercise 4

1. Who's; up; in
2. to; stationery
3. with; to
4. to
5. inferred; emigrated
6. advice

CHAPTER EIGHT

Plug In

1. his writing talent
2. consensus; stubborn
3. Now
4. spitting
5. SAT

Exercise 1

1. Our personalities are shaped by both heredity and environment.
2. Willis works full time, coaches Little League, gardens every weekend, and writes articles for his local newspaper.
3. Harry is a man with the best intentions and the highest principles.
4. (correct as is)
5. Neither the pleas of the editorial writers nor the threats of the demonstrators affected Judge Solomon's decision.

Exercise 2

1. She seems reclusive.
2. He asked about the expensive tour package.
3. Please consider Buddy's speech.
4. He got there by car. (Extra credit: He drove.)

Exercise 3

father

house

together with

dog

move to

cried

Exercise 4

Answers may vary.

At the end of October, I had to make a decision about my job. Since my boss was willing to discuss my options with me, I approached her about my plans. She is a woman who has high ethical standards and respect for the people in the company. "The majority of the projects here are temporary," she said reluctantly. "My bosses have me trapped: I don't want to lose you, but I don't want you to think mistakenly that there will still be work for you in six months' time. Because you have worked well with your colleagues, your supervisors, and your support staff, I think that you will be better off going elsewhere."

Glossary of Terms

Abstract Noun A noun that names an idea, a state of being, or a quality; a concept that has no physical reality.

Action Word (see *Verb*)

Adjective A word that describes or modifies a noun.

Adverb A word that describes or modifies a verb, adjective, or other adverb.

Antecedent The noun a pronoun replaces or stands in for.

Appositive A noun that is inserted into a sentence, usually right after another noun, renaming or identifying the first noun (differs from a noun complement because no linking verb intervenes to join the two nouns).

Articles The three small words (*a, an, the*) that function as modifiers or limiters of nouns by telling us whether the noun refers to a specific (particular) thing (*the* pineapple) or just one of those things in general (*a* pineapple, *an* orange).

Case The different forms pronoun take to reflect the role they are playing at that moment.

Clause A group of words containing both a subject and verb; may be either independent or dependent.

Cliché A figure of speech or a common phrase that has been overused to the point of becoming trite.

Collective Noun A noun that names a group of people or things (*family*, *jury*, *class*).

Common Noun A noun that names a class or type of person, place, thing or idea.

Complement A word or phrase used after the verb to complete the sense of the sentence; can be another noun, which *identifies* or *renames* the subject (Elvira was *his sister*) or a modifier, which *describes* the subject (*Ansel* is *fascinating*).

Concrete Noun A noun that names something that has a physical reality, that can be perceived with the senses (sight, sound, smell, taste, touch): the *dog*, a *computer*, the *skyscraper*, the *blare* of the radio, the *odor* of onions, the *wind* (*wind* might seem abstract, but you can *feel* it and sometimes *hear* it).

Contraction A word made by combining two other and using an apostrophe to show where letters have been omitted: *I am = I'm*.

Declarative Sentence One that makes a statement: *I like ice cream*.

Exclamatory Sentence One that expresses surprise or strong emotion: *What a drag!*

Fragment A piece of a sentence; a phrase or a dependent clause masquerading as complete sentence. *She wanted from him.*

Gerund A word ending in *-ing* that is formed from a verb but acts as a noun.

Helping Verb Forms of verbs that go with a main verb to indicate tense or mood or voice: I *am* running for office; *Do* you like the rookie catcher?; He *would have* preferred not to stay out so late.

Idiom A phrase or expression that is peculiar to itself; though it is part of the standard language, its meaning cannot be understood by combining the literal meanings of its individual words.

Imperative Sentence One that gives a command: *Pass the potatoes.*

Infinitive A form of the verb that consists of *to* + *the verb stem*; an infinitive can function as a noun, adjective, or adverb.

> *To err* is human; *to forgive* divine. (nouns)

> She thought this was a good place *to begin*. (adjective modifying the noun place)

> He coughed *to indicate* that he wanted to leave. (adverb modifying the verb coughed)

-*ing* Word (see *Gerund*; see *Participle, present*)

Interrogative Sentence One that asks a question. *How do you get to Carnegie Hall?*

Intransitive Verb One that expresses an action that is not transmitted to an object. Jody *sleeps* a lot when she travels.

Jargon Technical terminology used within a trade, profession, or similar group.

Linking Verb One that links the subject of the sentence with a complement (see *Complement*). She *is* pretty.

Noun Word used for naming something (person, place, thing, idea, emotion, etc.). See also *Abstract, Concrete, Proper, Common*.

Modifiers Words or phrases that modify or describe nouns, verbs, or adverbs.

Object The noun or pronoun that the verb does something *to* (Yvonne mailed the *letter*.). Can be direct or indirect. Also, a noun or pronoun after a preposition is the object of the preposition.

Parallel Structure The use of similar grammatical or syntactical forms to express similar ideas (in other words, if there's a pattern, follow it).

Participle A verb form that can function as part of a verb phrase (She *was laughing*) or as an adjective; present participles always end in *-ing*. (the *smiling* man, the *raving* lunatic); past participles end in either *-ed* or an *irregular* ending (the *tired* mother, the *torn* jacket).

Phrasal Verb A verb whose stem consists of one or more prepositions following the verb and acting as an integral part of the verb (to *pick on*, to *put up with*).

Phrase A group of related words that does not have a subject and a verb.

Preposition A word that shows the relationship (often of place or time) between things (Put the cake *on* a plate. Jo Ellen went *to* Paris.)

Pronoun A word that takes the place of, or stands in for, a noun (he, she, it).

Proper Noun One that names a unique or specific person, place, thing, or idea; proper nouns are always capitalized in English.

Redundancy A phrase that unnecessarily repeats itself or some part of its meaning: His hair is *red in color*.

Reflexive Pronoun A pronoun ending in *self* or *selves* (*yourself*, *myself*).

Run-On Sentence One in which two independent clauses are run together without adequate signals (punctuation, a word, or a combination of punctuation and a word) to notify the reader that one thought has ended and another has begun.

Sentence The expression of a complete and independent thought; it usually has a subject and a verb, but special types of sentences may not.

1. *Stop!* is an imperative sentence; it has only a verb, but the subject is implied: *You stop!*

2. *Why?* is an interrogatory sentence (a question), but the subject and verb are implied by whatever the previous speaker has said. ("I canceled the reservation," Daisy said. "*Why?*" asked Dimitri.)

3. *Good grief!* Aside from being Charlie Brown's favorite expression, this is an exclamation; it's an expression of emotion and does not need a subject and a verb.

Subject The actor in a sentence; the person, place, thing, idea that does (or is) something in a sentence.

Subjunctive The form of the verb that expresses a wish or a conditional statement (I wish the game *were* over. If Andrea *were* the principal, the school would be better off).

Tense The aspect of a verb that indicates the time or state of the action. (Present tense: I golf. Past tense: I golfed.)

Transitive verb A verb expressing action that takes an object (Emma *mailed* the letter).

Verb A word used to show action or a state of being.

Principal Parts of Irregular Verbs
(With a Special Feature on *Lay* and *Lie*)

Almost everyone has problems with some of the irregular verbs. The more you use them correctly, however, the more familiar they'll begin to sound. Try reading them aloud to reinforce the correct forms.

When you're not sure which form is correct, refer to this list or look up the verb in a dictionary (all good dictionaries list the principal parts of irregular verbs).

(The *present participle* is not included in this list because it is always the *-ing* form of the verb stem.)

Verb Stem (infinitive)	Past Tense	Past Participle
bear	bore	borne
become	became	become
begin	began	begun
bite	bit	bitten
blow	blew	blown
break	broke	broken
bring	brought	brought
build	built	built
burst	burst	burst
buy	bought	bought
catch	caught	caught
choose	chose	chosen
cling	clung	clung
come	came	come

Verb Stem (infinitive)	Past Tense	Past Participle
dive	dived (or dove)	dived
do	did	done
drag	dragged	dragged
draw	drew	drawn
drink	drank	drunk
drive	drove	driven
drown	drowned	drowned
eat	ate	eaten
fall	fell	fallen
fly	flew*	flown
forgive	forgave	forgiven
freeze	froze	frozen
fling	flung	flung
get	got	got/gotten
give	gave	given
go	went	gone
grow	grew	grown
hide	hid	hidden
hold	held	held
hurt	hurt	hurt
know	knew	known
lead	led	led
light	lit	lit
ride	rode	ridden
ring	rang	rung
rise	rose	risen
sew	sewed	sewn
shake	shook	shaken
shine (meaning glow)	shone	shone
shine (meaning polish)	shined	shined
shrink	shrank	shrunk

Verb Stem (infinitive)	Past Tense	Past Participle
sing	sang	sung
sink	sank (sunk)	sunk
speak	spoke	spoken
spin	spun	spun
spring	sprang	sprung
steal	stole	stolen
swear	swore	sworn
swim	swam	swum
swing	swung	swung
take	took	taken
tear	tore	torn
wake	woke/waked	waked
wear	wore	worn
write	wrote	written

*Except in baseball: "He flied out"; "He has flied out twice already."

LAY AND LIE

The verbs *to lay* and *to lie* are probably the two most confusing verbs in English. Because they are so widely used they are worth paying a little extra attention to.

To Lay or *to Lie*?

Present Stem	Past Tense	Past Participle	Present Participle
[to] lay	laid	laid	laying
[to] lie	lay	lain	lying

To lay means to put or place something down. It always takes an object. If you can substitute the verb *put* in your sentence you need a form of the verb *to lay*.

I *lay* the book on the table.

Yesterday I *laid* the book on the table.

I had just *laid* the book on the table when the phone rang.

I'm *laying* the book on the table.

To lie means to rest, relax, or place oneself in a horizontal position. It does not take an object. If you can substitute a form of the verb *recline* in your sentence, you need a form of the verb *to lie*.

I *lie* on the floor for fifteen minutes every afternoon.

Yesterday I *lay* on the floor for fifteen minutes.

I have *lain* on the floor for fifteen minutes every afternoon as long as I can remember.

I'm *lying* on the floor for fifteen minutes (so don't bother me).

Which is correct?
1. The books are (*lying, laying*) on the table.
2. Please (*lay, lie*) these coats across my bed for now.
3. Bernard has (*laid, lain*) in bed all day; I wonder if he's sick.

Use Your Substitute Words:
1. The books are *putting* on the table. (NO)
   The books are *reclining* on the table. (YES)

2. Please *put* these coats across my bed for now. (YES)
   Please *recline* these coats across my bed for now. (NO)

3. Bernard *has put* in bed all day . . . (NO)
   Bernard *has reclined* in bed all day . . . (YES)

Therefore, the answers are:
1. The books are *lying* on the table.
2. Please *lay* these coats across my bed for now.
3. Bernard has *lain* in bed all day; I wonder if he's sick.

Power Sources

When you want more information about grammar, usage, punctuation, or language itself, try one or more of the following:

The Elements of Style. William Strunk, Jr., and E. B. White. 3rd ed. New York: Macmillan, 1979.

English Grammar Simplified. Blanche Ellsworth and John A. Huggins. New York: HarperCollins, 1992.

The Language Instinct. Steven Pinker. New York: Morrow, 1994.

Merriam Webster's Guide to Punctuation and Style. Springfield, Massachusetts: Merriam-Webster. 1995

Woe is I: The Grammarphobe's Guide to Better English in Plain English. Patricia T. O'Conner. New York: Grosset/Putnam, 1996.

And, of course, keep a good dictionary on hand.